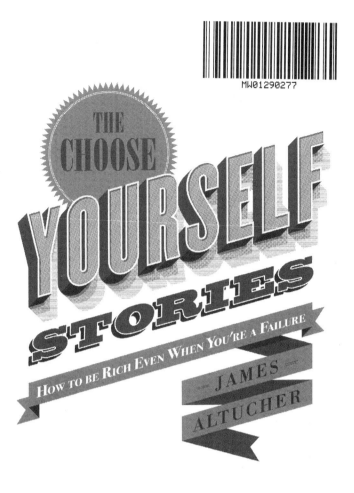

THE CHOOSE YOURSELF STORIES

HOW TO BE RICH EVEN WHEN YOU'RE A FAILURE

JAMES ALTUCHER

ISBN-13: 978-1500193416   ISBN-10: 1500193410

Printed in the United States of America
Cover design by: Herb Thornby/Erin Tyler
Interior design by: Erin Tyler

DEDICATION

To Claudia, who chose me.

TABLE OF CONTENTS

Foreword To The *Choose Yourself Stories*............................ 8

How To Be A Superhero.. 16

Fearless Blogging... 20

My First Customer is Now Dead.. 24

Don't Go To Jail.. 30

How To Be An Ultimate Fighter... 36

How I Killed Osama Bin Laden.. 42

How To Avoid Death... 46

How To Be A TV Star.. 50

How To Get Rich, The Push... 54

I Want To Live... 58

How To Be The King Of The World..................................... 60

There's No Painless Way to Kill Yourself............................ 64

The Day I Stopped a Ten Million Dollar Robbery.................. 68

With All Due Respect..74

Three Card Monte For Your Soul...78

Imaginary Letter From My Teenage Daughter to Me...........84

Girl With The Name That Was a Curse...............................88

Prostitutes, Drugs, HBO, and the Best Job I Ever Had..........92

Live Sex, Chess, and Shame..96

The Day Stockpickr Was Going to Go Out of Business –

A Story of Friendship...101

My Blind Date Gone Bad...106

Hitchhiker's Guide to the Universe...................................110

How to Win at Monopoly Every Time...............................114

My Visit To The White House..118

Go With The Flow: I'm A Lucky Guy................................122

Everything Is Funny All The Time....................................126

How Stevie Cohen Changed My Life.................................130

Did I Mention I was Once a Respiratory Therapist?...........136

My New Year Resolution in 1995.....................................142

The One Reason Why Facebook is Worth $100 Billion......146

How I Screwed Yasser Arafat Out of $2 Million................150

I'm Guilty of Torturing Women..158

How to Succeed In LA Without Really Trying...................162

Imagine You Are Ten Years Old......................................166

When I Was Completely Humiliated By Yoga....................170

My Name is James A and I'm an Alcoholic.......................174

My Lawyer is Dead...180

I Want My Kids to Be Drug Addicts................................184

I Want to Be Like Google When I Grow Up.....................188

Live Your Life As If Everyone Else Was Going to
Die Today...194

Make Every Moment a Work of Art................................198

Obsession...202

Steve Wynn and the Lost Diamonds of Africa..................206

140Love- The Ultimate Dating Service............................210

Freedom...216

I Want My Daughters to be Lesbians..............................222

How I Met Claudia..224

Falling in Love..230

I Hope to God I don't Repeat the Past............................234

How I Disappointed Tupac's Mom.................................238

I Am The Bravest Man Alive...242

I'm Ashamed...246

I Had To Lie...248

Three Stories About Billionaires.....................................252

Why a Grenade Needs to Get Thrown at Me...................256

The Year I Did Nothing But Play Poker.............................. 260

How to Be a Comedian...264

Mouse In The Salad...270

Why I Started Stockpickr.. 274

Lots of Naked People... 280

About The Author..286

FOREWORD TO THE CHOOSE YOURSELF STORIES

I was walking on the street and I stepped in some dog crap and had to wipe it off my shoes.

Scraping my shoes on the staircase of the browstone I was right outside of. Then the door opens and the guy comes out and yells, "hey, what the hell are you doing?" and he starts jumping down the stairs. I ran away and didn't look back for about three blocks.

It's one of those things where it was my fault but it wasn't my fault.

I mean, I was wiping the dog crap off of his steps. I was basically outsourcing my problem to him. Which was bad.

But it was instinct. As soon as I stepped in it (which, by law, someone should've cleaned) I started wiping it off. Wouldn't anyone do that?

So that's what this book is about: When life happens and it's your fault and it's not your fault. But told through stories that happened to me.

Life is pretty hard. We're given a very tightly defined comfort zone to live in. Notice we all dress basically the same.

We all eat roughly the same foods. In fact, 68 million members of the human species are eating at a McDonalds today.

(As a sidenote: I should mention that a lot of fun facts like that will be literally littered throughout this book.)

Many of us have had bad relationships, bad jobs. Bad bosses. Arguments with family and friends.

Life isn't fun. In fact, the hardest thing we've done is being born. It's a pretty difficult world, hurtling through space and dodging asteroids and mini-black holes, amongst all the other things we have to deal with.

I don't like it.

All of these things: the plans we have for our futures, the hopes and dreams we work really hard towards, are the walls we build of our comfort zone. We think we can construct a dome of safety to avoid all pain. For example, get the degree, get the spouse, get the job, get the kids, get the house, build the savings, retire comfortably, have a healthy retirement, die. This is one example of a comfort zone we are all taught to respect and even worship.

To stay within that comfort zone we have to do A LOT of unpleasant work starting from about age six.

And often walls within that comfy little mental palace we build start to break down. Maybe we get fired from the job. Or we lose the house. Or the partner betrays us. Or the kids don't like us.

I don't know. A lot of it seems like practice for me. We practice living life as a human so that we can then hopefully go on to better things.

I wrote the book "Choose Yourself" because I had a hard time choosing myself. That's why most people write books. Because you learn an enormous amount about failure. You learn so much that hopefully you figure out some ways to overcome those failures and move past them.

I hope I was able to learn how to "Choose myself" and based on the emails I have gotten in the past year I can see that many people put into process the same ideas that helped me.

But for a long time I really messed up. I kept destroying my comfort zone and it wasn't fun.

Charles Darwin said that wild animals have bigger brains than domesticated animals.

I didn't want to be domesticated anymore.

This doesn't mean become homeless or live in the woods.

All it means is: I want to learn, every day, how to accept my surroundings, how to do the things I want to do, be with the people I want to be with, and accept the fact that I can't control my future. The universe is an infinite place and doesn't have to be limited by the comfort zone instilled in me by my own fears, by the fears of others, by the demands of others, by the wants of others.

If you don't choose yourself, someone else will and the result won't be pleasant. If you don't live in the world of choosing, you live in the world of excusing.

Some of these stories are embarrassing. But I hope you will relate to some of them and see that if someone like me can start to move down this path of breaking down the comfort zone and seeing the infinite that is out there, then you can also.

I hate using that phrase "the infinite that is out there". But it's true. It's ours for the taking, for the exploring, and maybe it's just more fun. It's much better than trying to constantly satisfy a thirst that can't be satisfied.

Never forget that your well is already full. You and I are alive. And for the person who is still thirsty when the well is full, that person's thirst will be unquenchable.

I hope this book will help satisfy your thirst.

[I am going to try a marketing technique a friend of mine told me. "Put in the Amazon sample of your book a link to your email list". So I will do it. My email list has a lot more stories than I put on my blog. And I feel a good community is developing among the people on my list.

ANOTHER FOREWORD TO THE CHOOSE YOURSELF STORIES

Hmmm, I wrote that first foreword but maybe I have a little more to say.

I'm going to die soon.

And by soon, I mean sometime between a second from now and about 100 years from now.

I was visiting with a friend of mine who got worried that everyone will be downloading their souls into computers by the year 2045. Ray Kurzweil, the proponent of an idea called "the singularity", personally told my friend this. "2045 he said," he said.

First off, no they won't.

Second, it doesn't matter to me. I'm not going to do it. I want to live life to the fullest this very moment. Not inside of a computer. "But what if the hospitals force you to be downloaded?"

Ok, ok. No they won't. Enough of this already.

I've lost a lot of money repeatedly. I wrote about that in "Choose Yourself". I also wrote how we are living in a time of greater economic uncertainty, even societal uncertainty than ever and I gave the reasons why.

I also wrote about how I personally deal with that uncertainty and why and how I could be optimistic. Not necessarily optimistic about fantasy futures. I don't like to live in fantasies. But just optimistic. As whooshy as this sounds, I like to feel good. Right now.

Part of what was making me feel not so good as I was always relying for many years on others to choose me. Maybe at an emotional level: parents, friends, lovers. Maybe at a career level: bosses, institutions, a book publisher, a TV producer. Someone, anyone who could CHOOSE us and validate our parking and make us feel better about our place on the planet.

I wanted to choose myself. So I could define where and why and how I go on this planet before everything I know is extinguished like the tiny flame that sits atop a match.

So I wrote the book. But along the way I left out a lot of stories. Because the book was not intended to be a book of stories. It was intended to help and while storytelling is often the best way to deliver a message, the book itself wasn't about storytelling.

This one is. This is the best book I've ever written. I am so proud of the stories in this book I...I don't know. I'm just really proud of them.

About 25 years ago I started writing fiction. I would write 3000 words a day.

I was a computer programmer, so I took a job where I wrote a program and all I had to do was maintain it. Since the program worked, I spent almost all of my time writing and reading.

I wrote several novels. Notable titles among these novels include: "The Porn Novelist, the Romance Novelist, the Prostitute, and They're Lovers", "The Book of Orpheus", "The Book of David" (you see I liked that semi-Biblical "Book of"), and "Chess Pieces" (get it - stories about people who play chess.).

I wrote many short stories and sent them to every magazine.

Everything I ever wrote got rejected. All form letters. Not even a letter saying, "keep at it. You're pretty good and one day you will be better."

Maybe that was for the best because I gave up after about 4 years and moved to New York City and began to have many adventures. I write about many of these adventures here in this book.

But I think that was the beginning of my training as a writer. To write 3000 words a day for four or five years. Then I wrote stuff for HBO and then I began an eight or nine year stint writing for financial publications.

I started writing dry stuff. Like about stocks. But then one day the editor in chief of the Financial Times summoned me to his office and basically said, "if you don't start getting a little crazy in your column we're going to get rid of it."

I'm really grateful for that advice. I started getting a little crazy. And then I got even crazier. I finally started saying what I felt I really wanted to say. And I did that for many years. And, I'm not afraid to say it, I think I got better. I think I was really bad at first but finally I got to the point where I can say, "I have no clue what I'm doing". Which is a hard but honest place to be.

And that's why I'm really proud of what you are about to read. Because I have no clue. But sometimes it's fun to be a wild animal.

THIRD FOREWORD

I'm really not intending this as a joke. To write foreword after foreword.

But I just noticed that the top bestselling book according to the New York Times this week is a book called "Heaven is for Real" about a boy who "died" for a few minutes and then comes back and describes what heaven looks like.

How come a little 6 year old kid never dies and then is miraculously revived and says, "Holy FF&&&! You WOULD NOT BELIEVER THE SH*&ST&RM I just saw. HELL IS REAL!" And then that kid could write a bestselling book. The books could vie for the #1 bestselling position on the bestseller lists.

Anyway.

I hope you like my book.

HOW TO BE A SUPERHERO

I lied to him to get a job. The hedge fund manager asked me how much money I had in the bank.

I had ZERO but I said, "a million dollars". This was in 2002.

In the prior two years I had lost all the money I ever made and my home. Now I was broke.

He said, "how can you afford to live on that?"

Which strikes me as ludicrous now but I felt every blood cell in me turn upside down in shame then.

I felt he would think it was courageous if I threw the question back at him.

"Well, how much money do you have?"

He said, "one hundred million dollars." Who knows?

One friend of mine told me something, "you can never tell how much money someone has until they file for bankruptcy."

I read a statistic that people lie (including "white lies"), on average, 10-200 times a day. I also read that people say, on average, 2500 words a day.

So one technique to stop lying is to stop talking. I try not to talk. I try to say around 1000 words a day.

The hedge fund manager and I then went out to dinner with

his wife. He was cheating on his wife but I didn't know that yet.

I had read all his favorite books so I was able to quote from them. "What are your favorite books?" he said. I quoted from those books (Ayn Rand bullshit). Then I quoted from a research paper he wrote in 1969 that I had found buried in some journal.

He asked me, "What are my interests outside of finance?" I knew he liked baseball so I talked about various histories of baseball I had just read. Baseball is boring.

The hedge fund manager gave me money to manage. It was my first "job" in the financial space. In a very short time I more than doubled the money he had given me.

A year or so later I wrote a book about how I did it. He instantly fired me. He thought I had revealed too much. He wrote, "our financial relationship is now over."

I wrote, "it's not. You owe me money because I have made you so much." So he instantly sent a check.

One day, I had to return my dad's car to the dealership. My dad had a stroke and was in a coma and would never drive a car again. After I dropped it off the hedge fund manager called me and invited me to dinner.

I went to the dinner and started drinking quite a bit. I was feeling depressed.

To my right was the mistress. And in front of me was the hedge fund manager's daughter.

I was shy and had a crush on the daughter and so I blurted out the only question I could think of, "so what do you think of [manager] and [mistress] being so out in the open?"

[Daughter] looked at [mistress] and said, "I think she is a money hungry slut." And then she got up and walked out of the restaurant.

I was horrified and embarrassed. [The wife] even wrote me the next day and was upset at me and [manager] was upset at me until finally I said to everyone, "this is your family issue. I have my own family issues."

Anyway, my book came out right after that and I was fired.

All of this is to say, better to speak fewer words.

Less lies, more time to listen and learn and think and daydream. Less embarrassing situations.

Less masks to wear. My mental closet can only fit so many masks. The older I get, the less masks fit in that closet.

More benefits of not opening your mouth: flies dont get in your mouth. Less food gets in your mouth so you eat better.

You give less advice. Nobody listens to my advice anyway. People do what they want until they are injured like a kid putting his fingers on the stove.

Telling the truth is easier. It means you just have to remember things.

Telling a lie means you have to remember, AND THEN keep track of the lie. Too much stress! (Polygraph machines, in fact, work by measuring stress levels).

Less "mouth" means you start to use your eyes and ears more. Like the way blind people can hear and touch better.

Blind people seem to develop super powers with their other senses.

People who talk less are like superheroes in the same way.

If you become a superhero and see me lying homeless in the gutter, please save me.

FEARLESS BLOGGING

I thought I was going to drive over a little baby that was crawling across the street.

"What little baby?" my driving instructor said.

Well, what IF there was a little baby? And what if I don't brake?

"Why wouldn't you brake?"

So many questions! It's hard to drive a 2 ton metallic vehicle at 70 miles an hour in an empty school parking lot. And then go on a highway for the first time. And then parallel park!

There could be babies anywhere. Why WOULDN'T there be a baby trying to crawl across the street?

The driving instructor, who was my dad, looked ahead. At some point he said something about kids in Soviet Russia. I don't know. I wasn't paying attention. I had to focus on the babies.

Why are you driving so slowly? My dad asked me.

Didn't he understand the danger?

Now, of course, I regularly kill babies while I'm driving at 70 miles per hour, while simultaneously drinking my coffee and texting on my phone, and I don't even notice.

100s of babies. I get points when I kill babies. I win the game when I kill babies.

Who even cares if I kill all the babies that are crawling all over the highway. I still see them in my mind's eye. They are everywhere.

But I have enough experience to know now that when I run over them by the dozens that nobody will care, nobody will notice, nobody will ever miss the babies.

It's the same thing with blogging.

I'm scared to hit a baby when I write a post. Ever since my first post, I don't hit "Publish" unless I'm scared.

Someone asked me the other day what I thought of a particular blog post written by some random guy. I looked at it and thought it was very bad.

The writer had a lot of ego. He started off bragging about his accomplishments. Then he gave a "top 10 blah blah" like "top 10 ways to be the best you can be" or something like that. But he didn't give any personal stories.

I want to know when the blogger was the WORST he ever was. The absolute WORST. And what technique he used to get over it.

Maybe he should start, "I only felt truly alive when smoking crack with homeless girls" and the steps he took so he could feel truly alive in other situations, like when he was eating oatmeal by himself.

I want to learn how to not be lonely.

I want to know how to feel at peace when my heart is racing in anger over something she said, or he did, or they wanted. Or how to be calm when my bank account is going down. Or how to think "yes" when the people I want to love me tell me "no".

I want to learn how to make better decisions. So I don't end up in a gutter with a needle sticking out of my eyeball.

I want to know how to feel alive!

When Kamal told me he was nervous about writing his book, nervous about what people would think of him, I told him, I ONLY write when I am nervous about what people will think. Then he wrote my favorite book.

And people will THINK. Believe me.

People will think I'm a bad parent. Or a loser. Or I used to write better.

Or people will say "James is a scam". Or people will say "his writing is ADHD" whatever that means. Or they will say "he just tries to provoke" or people will say "he's a criminal" or people will say "why do they even let him live" or sometimes they will say to me (yesterday) "you have asshole powers" or people will say (yesterday) "you look like a jackass".

And I get afraid. Will this post be better than the last? Will it be my best ever or my worst ever? Am I revealing too much? Am I helping people? Am I helping people but still telling a story? Is it a good story?

I'm scared every time I sit down to write. I'm ashamed every time I hit "publish".

500 posts in... What if I run out of stories? What if I run out of things to say? Will I jump the shark?

"James Altucher rubs me the wrong way! I HATE him."

Why!? I don't understand. What did I do?

I hit "Publish".

MY FIRST CUSTOMER IS
NOW DEAD

I was lonely and I wanted money. I was living in a one-bedroom apartment in Astoria, Queens, NYC in 1995. I knew nobody in the area. I would write my phone number on two dollar bills and tip waitresses with them. Nobody called me. Everyone in Astoria is Greek. And they pretty much stick to themselves.

Nobody would talk to me. I would walk for miles in Astoria hoping that just one person would talk to me.

Weekends were the worst. I missed my friends at work. The Museum of the Moving Image was down the street so I would go there to watch various indie movies. Two things: the Hal Hartley retrospective was great. And the collection of Bill Cosby sweaters that he wore in his 80s show was prominently on display. The woman taking the tickets didn't like me because I always flashed my HBO ID to get in free.

I had about $20 in the bank and lived paycheck to paycheck. I would walk around every part of Manhattan and think to myself, "who are the millions of people who can afford to live here but I can't?"

Adrian called me. "I have to do this diamond website, can you help?" We went over to Shlomo's on 47th Street. Shlomo told me that all the diamonds on 47th Street get smuggled into the US to avoid taxes.

I asked him how they get smuggled. He said, "I will tell you a joke

"Two jews are coming back from Russia. One keeps squirming the whole plane ride. The other jew finally asks him, 'Moishe, why all the squirming?

"Moishe says, 'Because I'm sorting the inventory!' "

Shlomo laughed. Adrian laughed. I thought to myself, I am never going to buy a diamond.

Shlomo wanted to put online his wholesale business which he used to sell to all the diamond dealers on 47th Street (known in NYC as the diamond district. If you walk down 47th Street its all tourists and Hasidic Jews) and sell direct to the consumer. "I don't want my name anywhere on this! If anyone on the street knew I was doing this they would kill me." Arguably this would be the first diamond site on the Internet. Before Blue Nile, before Tiffany's went online. Before anything.

He gave us a file that was his entire database. Every diamond was one line on the file with all the features separated by commas. The shape of the diamond, the 4Cs (cut, clarity, carats, color), the number of the GIA certificate (since certification is the universal scam, even diamonds have to be certified by some bogus organization). He just wanted the database online and a simple design. People would select a diamond on the site and then send him an email and he would call them. Simple.

My room in Astoria had one foam mattress in it, cockroaches in the bathroom, a phone, and a black and white TV about 3 inches diagonal that never worked. I didn't realize that in

NYC you needed cable to get a TV to work. I had no chairs, no sheets, no plates or glasses, no food, no closet, no dressers, and kept all of my clothes in a garbage bag. Even if a waitress spoke to me, what was I going to do? I felt worthless. I needed the money.

The next day Chet called me and asked me what I was up to. I told him about the diamond project. "What programming language are you going to use?" I told him I thought I would use C++ but I wasn't sure. I figured it would take me about a month with C++.

"James, James, nononono," he said, "trust me on this. Go to the bookstore. G-g-g-get O'Reilly's book on PERL. Trust me." Chet had a slight stutter when he was excited. His mind was too fast for his words.

"What's PERL?"

"Just trust me. Get the book. Then call me."

I got the book, went into Adrian's office and set up a simple Perl programming environment (downloadable from a dozen sources). Did the basic "Hello, world" program. Kept flipping through the book.

I called Chet later that day. "Did you get the book?" he asked.

"I finished the whole project," I said. I even added an extra flourish. I found a Perl library for manipulating graphic images so I used it to create the GIA certificates on the fly as images. Perl became my favorite programming language for all Internet projects back then.

LESSONS:

- Learn a programming language quickly by modifying other code. I found code for searching a database. I just modified that and fed in this database. As long as you know the basic tools: if, then, loops, recursion, the syntax of the language,

functions, etc you can learn any programming language by
having a book for the basic syntax and modifying other code

- Always add an extra flourish. ALWAYS. No matter what.
  This was my first client. Of the next five jobs I did, three
  of them offered me a full time job with double or triple the
  salary I was making at HBO. It's because I always delivered
  that extra something. This is more than "underpromise and
  overdeliver". This is using creativity to make the client's
  life better. And to always have the element of surprise. They
  know that when you walk in the door magic will happen,
  doves will fly. I was the magician.
- Always talk to someone smarter than you are and get their
  advice on how to do a job.

We delivered to Shlomo. He couldn't believe how fast we did
it. He couldn't believe we also did the GIA certificates the way
we did. He gave us more work.

He paid us in cash. $35,000. I took, $17,500.

I walked over to The Chelsea Hotel on 23rd Street and said
I wanted to move in. They were known for only letting artists
and writers live there. Arthur C Clarke wrote "2001: A Space
Odyssey" there. Madonna wrote "Sex" there. Dylan Thomas
died on the steps leading in. Nancy was stabbed there ("Sid
and Nancy"). I was told to wait for Stanley Bard to see me. He
owned the hotel. I waited for two hours and then he took me
into the office. I gave him the $17,500 in cash and asked if I
could live there for a year.

He looked at the cash. It was in a paper bag from a supermarket, in hundreds. "What are you," he said, "a drug dealer?"
I should've added, the Chelsea Hotel was known for letting
artists, writers, and drug dealers live there. And high-end
prostitutes. And some not very high-end. I didn't want to say

I worked on the Internet. That was very uncool back then. It meant I was a "computer geek". Not good.

I said, "I work at HBO."

"Ok," he said. And he took me up to the first floor, to the right, to the room where Nancy was stabbed (it had been divided into two rooms by then). "You can stay here," he said. I later moved several times to different parts of the building. Every floor in the Chelsea had its own little subculture. I felt like an anthropologist as I moved up the different floors, studying the species that inhabited each floor. There was art hanging everywhere. All of the art was awful.

Recently, Adrian called me. He was still working on the site, diamondcutters.com. I think even now he's still working on it. "Shlomo is dead," he said. "What happened?" I said.

"He was flying a plane around Russia. I guess looking for diamonds. The plane crashed."

I thought of Shlomo's joke about the squirming jew flying back from Russia. I thought how Shlomo never really liked me. In 1999 I talked him into paying a million dollars to theknot. com to become the exclusive diamond dealer on their site but it resulted in almost no sales for him. He never spoke to me again after that.

I thought of the girl who worked in his office who had the huge scar down one side of her face. I thought of how I loved her and wanted to lick her scar and be the only one to tell her how beautiful she was.

Shlomo's dead. I'm alive.

DON'T GO TO JAIL

I don't think any of the prostitutes were above the age of 18. One girl told me she was sixteen. They were all black. The 16 year old was laughing and sort of skipping around while she was talking to me.

They were waiting for the bus to return from Riker's Island, the prison. This particular bus stop was like a bloody, inflected gash at the bottom of Queens. We were the fleas fiiling it. The last street at the end of the world.

This was the only stop for the bus out of Riker's Island and it went back and forth all night. Anyone just-bailed out would get drugs from the drug dealers and whatever they could from the prostitutes.

It was a crazy poem that rhymed all night. This was their day.

I was talking to a sixteen year old girl about why she was doing this. She was wearing skin tight clothes, short shorts, a tank top that hugged her so fierce it was like part of her skin.

She had small breasts and depending on how she moved, one of her nipples would peek out.

"Doing what?" she said. She couldn't stop smiling, skipping, a tiny dance.

A guy stepped between her and me, tattoos up and down his tank-topped arms, flashed teeth filled with gold, silver, and dark red gums at me, then turned to her.

I didn't see what he did to her although they were no more than two feet from me. I heard an "ooomph" from her. "OOOmph!" An exhalation of air like a bullet shot out of her mouth.

She folded in half and fell to the ground. Then she got up and limped very slowly around the corner into the darkest crevice of the brutal maze we were in. I couldn't go around the corner. It was pitch black there. And when I peeked one time later there were dark shapes just shifting around.

There was a Mini-Donuts shop at the corner. A greasy bright light with yellow walls and Indian workers looking skeptically at the customers, even me.

Construction workers were everywhere, wearing their bright orange and yellow fluorescent jackets so cars wouldn't run them over. One of the construction guys came up to me and said, "don't worry. We're the police. If you need anything, let us know." Somehow I was under the cone of protection. I was working on a project for HBO. I wore my HBO jacket.

One time I stood with a mother and her daughter. They were waiting for the bus to arrive. "We have to go bail out my son," the mother said to me. What did he do, I asked. He did nothing, she said.

What had burned straight through their brains, making their eyes look like candy? If your brains had been ironed through like that would your eyes taste the same?

We all got on the bus. I sat in the back with a woman who was a cop. "I'm going to retire in a year," she said. "I want to move to Florida and be a massage therapist." I could believe it. She had thick arms. She could crush me in a massage. She was thick everywhere.

I went up front and sat next to the bus driver. He was bald and had a face like the back of a tack with two eyes.

"I do this every day, all night long," he told me. "Its always the same people going back and forth. I get my pension in ten years. The city of New York takes pretty good care of me. I ignore all the junkies but sometimes you see things on this job. I guess I'm going to do this every night for the next ten years. It ain't so bad. They take care of me."

We crossed over a bridge and now we were on Riker's Island. The entire island is the prison. "Sit in the back," the bus driver told me, "and put your cameras under the seat and put your coat over the cameras."

There was only one stop on the island. I said goodbye to the mother and daughter and wished them luck. In my arrogance I felt I could marry the daughter and save her. She wasn't pretty or ugly. She had a shy voice. She had plump fat all over her. She was protecting her mother.

We stopped at the only building with light coming out of it. It was the only light on the island and it blinded everyone on the bus. I watched the passengers disappear into that light, incinerating them.

Prison guards dragged a big white guy onto the bus. He couldn't move but they dragged him on and threw him onto the front seat. "Heavy," one of the guards said. The white guy slumped forward on his seat. He had a gut. A blue ripped t-shirt and jeans. A moustache. Bad acne on his forehead that was covered by greasy black hair.

A burn on his face and arm that looked like it could get infected. It had a red, fresh look – the burn still sparkled with different shades of dead skin.

The bus left the island. I sat next to the burn guy. "What happened to you?" He wouldn't answer.

"Hey buddy!" the bus driver said and tried to look around to see burn guy, "can you talk?" the burn guy wouldn't answer. "Can you talk?" a little louder. No answer.

"Uh oh," the bus driver said.

We got back to Long Island City. The burn guy was still slumped forward. Not talking. He didn't get off the bus after everyone else had left. His eyes were blinking. He briefly looked at me when I asked him if he was ok. But then he went back to just looking at the floor.

"Oh f*&^," the bus driver said. "I need some help here. I got a guy who won't get off the bus," he said into an intercom. "no, he's just not moving."

An ambulance showed up. I asked one of the guys from the ambulance what was wrong with the guy. "There's nothing wrong with him," he said, "and you're in my way."

It took about four of them to carry the guy off of the bus. They put him in the ambulance. I was standing right next to the ambulance and the burn guy was sitting up on the cot in there. The ambulance started its siren even though there was no traffic at this time and it drove off. I could see burn guy not moving and getting smaller as the ambulance drove off.

The burn guy was just going from one facility to another. 14 years later is he now a father? Do daughters now love him?

All the prostitutes and drug dealers were now gone or busy. The gray light of morning speckled onto the dirty avenue. Nobody was even in the mini-donuts shop.

"It's just another day. You can't let this stuff get to you," the bus driver told me. And he shut the door and and with a big shifting of gears and levers the bus pulled out of its stop and drove off, under the bridges and tracks that criss-crossed right above us – making sure all the cars and people from Long Island or Manhattan would always stay fifty feet higher.

Now I was by myself. I found myself missing the bus driver and even missing burn guy. But it was time for me to go back over the river and go home The sun was coming up.

Time for breakfast

How To Be An Ultimate Fighter

"This tube you see coming out of me is directly connected with my heart and pumps liquid into it, faking my heart into thinking it's ok."

The driver was talking to Brian and me. He had picked us up earlier today from the golf club where we had been playing hall-of-fame football player Dan Marino. We were skipping the charity dinner and using a car service to get back to the city.

I saw the tube sticking out of the driver's side and the liquids that seemed to be going from the tube to the bag next to him and asked if he was ok.

The answer was no.

"I need a heart transplant," he said. And then he explained the tube.

He said, "My heart is three times bigger than the average heart. It can't get enough oxygen. I can barely move."

"Jesus," I said, "how did this happen?"

We were driving up the turnpike. Brian and I were in the back. Dave, the driver was in the front.

David, the driver, said, "I wanted to be in the Ultimate Fighting Champtionships and so I took Ephedrine to get my weight down from 215 to 175."

What is that, I said, like a steroid?

No, Brian said, they used to sell it in GNC.

Did you take too much of it, I said.

I just took what the bottle said I should take, Dave said.

"Then I started getting this consistent flu so I went to the doctor. I was in great shape. The doctor said I was in impeccable health. That's the word he used. "Impeccable". Dave laughed.

"I had to look it up," he said, "it means perfect. I was muscle on top of muscle. I was ready to fight."

Then the doctor said, "But I don't know how to tell you this." I didn't know what he was going to say. I was just a little sick.

The doctor said, I don't think you're going to live.

"I have type two Diabetes now. I have high cholesterol. I have high blood pressure. I have a pacemaker on the left side of my heart and this Primacor tube on the right side. I can't deal with my diabetes because I can't bring my weight down enough without damaging my heart.

"What happens if you take that tube out?" I said.

"Within an hour I'll feel as if I have a really bad flu," he said. "And within a month or two I'll be dead."

"What if you kept the tube in," I said, "How long can you live?"

"I have to take the tube out anyway in three months," Dave

said, "Because the body gets too used to it and it doesn't do any good anymore. So after those three months I have one month to live.

"I have to go to the doctors Friday," he said, "but they refuse to see me now. Because a heart transplant costs over two million dollars and my house is being foreclosed on and I have no insurance. I have no money and even if I got a transplant I can't afford the anti-rejection pills that you have to take for the rest of your life to make sure the body accepts the new heart."

We were making our way over the GW Bridge. The traffic and 95 degree heat and sun and police blocks and all the confusing corners and intersections right around that crazy juncture between New Jersey and New York were slowing us down.

"This is depressing," he said, "let's talk about something else."

"Were you good at fighting?" I said. "When was the last fight you were in."

"Ever since I was seven I just loved putting my fist in someone's face. If someone hurt me, it was a guarantee I was going to hurt them harder. But I'm not like that anymore. Now I'm just grateful every second to be alive."

He said, "A few weeks ago I was at a bar with my friend. I had the tube tucked away in what I was wearing. Some guys started bothering my friend who was talking to a cute girl.

"So I asked them to stop. They started to get closer to me and I was moving back. They were huge and juiced up and I didn't know what was going to happen. To be honest, I should've left them alone because if they ripped this tube out I would have been in serious trouble. This tube is connected right into my heart.

"But I poked the main guy in the eye really hard. I just jabbed right in the center of the eye." He looked at me through the rear view mirror. "What would you do if someone jabbed you in the eye?" he said.

"I guess I would probably cry," I said.

"No," he said, "you'd put your hands on your eyes and you'd bend forward. That's what everyone does."

"Then, while the guy was bent forward, I hit at his adam's apple on his throat. I just did it lightly. If I had done it stronger I would've broken his windpipe. He was down on the ground and the bouncer threw him out. The whole thing took five seconds."

"How'd you learn to do that?"

"I've just been doing it all my life. When I was younger I studied boxing and all the martial arts. That's why I wanted to do ultimate fighting. But now I can't. Now I can't even go grocery shopping. I have to pay some kids to help me shop for food."

"I've been dead twice," he said, "And both times I felt like I was on an escalator that would slow down and reverse. And then I would wake up with doctors and nurses all around me and no memory of how I got there."

I'm just so happy, he said. I'm so happy to be alive.

"I've got a sixteen year old boy," Dave said. "I hope he's a success in life. That's all I want. I didn't really know my dad. He was murdered when I was five."

"What happened?" I said.

"I don't know," he said, "he wasn't living with us no more. So my mom and I went over to his house and all I remember is that there was blood everywhere. I remember that he had dark hair. Sometimes I look up at the sky and I hope he can hear me talking to him.

"And now," he said, "all I want is to see my son graduate. He graduates in 12 months. I hope everyone is wrong about my four or five months left to live. But right now this second, I am so grateful and happy to be here, to be alive, to be talking to you guys."

"What keeps you so optimistic?" I said.

"All of us here," he said, "are going to die. There's no exception. We are all going to die.

"So you have two choices. You can die crying or you can die smiling. I'm going to die smiling."

We were getting closer to where I had to be dropped off in the city where I was going to meet Claudia. We got a little lost thanks to my inability to ever give good directions. Finally we got to my destination.

"Well," he said, as I was getting out of the car. "I'm going to beat this thing, James. I'm going to come back when nobody said I could and I'm going to beat this thing and get my health back."

"I know you are, Dave. I really think you are."

But, in truth, I didn't.

How I Killed
Osama Bin Laden

I wanted to run out the back stairwell when they said they were from the police and wanted to talk to me. They flashed a badge on the security monitor.

They had those firm voices that some people with mustaches are born with.

The elevator came straight up into my apartment. The apartment I was losing because I went broke and could no longer afford the mortgage or the maintenance or the taxes or the food.

The babysitter took the kids into another room. I heard them laughing. She would tickle them and the giggles scratched my heart.

The elevator opened and they showed their badges again, but this time the badges said, "FBI".

"We only said 'Police' downstairs because we didn't want to scare people on the street," one of the guys said. Their voices made that logic seem irresistible.

"We have reason to believe you can tell us something about the finances of UBL," Person A said.

"UBL is Osama Bin-Laden", Person B said.

Apparently, Dr. Larry Brilliant (his real name and former head of Google Charities) mentioned to them a conversation I once had with him about bin Laden in 1999.

Larry had invested in a company I had started and destroyed during a period where I destroyed a lot of the things I touched. One time I said to Larry that a friend of mine worked at an investment firm that had money from the bin-Laden family.

My friend had said, "it's on all of their European brochures but none of their American brochures."

I told this to the FBI guys.

"Yeah, we've had our eyes on XYZ Partners for a long time. This is helpful."

They stuck around and had coffee and we shot pool on my antique 1948 pool table. The first brand of pool table that had automatic ball return.

Later that month, I had to sell the pool table to pay expenses.

"Can I ask," I said, "How come there haven't been any other terrorist attacks since 9/11?"

"Believe me," Person A said, "we've stopped quite a few."

Then they left.

And I was feeling relieved. So relieved. Like I had avoided chains and darkness for one more day.

Because I was guilty. The weight of the two of them in my house crushed me with strangulating guilt. I could barely breathe.

I don't know why I felt guilty. I write now to try and figure out why. To connect dots but the dots are always shifting.

I wanted my life to be different. Nothing added up anywhere. On the paper, on the screen, on the kaleidoscope of images that would pretend to be my day. I had been an addict in ways that, honest as I try to be, I can't say.

But enough to put me in jail in my head for 1000 years times

1000. My little baby would cry, the woman on the phone would cry, and I'll never be able to cheer her up.

It's hard to be human. People are cruel. The people you love are sent down to test you and it's a race to see who disappoints who first.

To scrape by and live is often humiliating and degrading. The things we do to tease out love we hide and bury like a dog would bury a dead rat.

Before we are discovered. Before we are found out and hunted down.

And then we create new humans. Somehow it happens. A simple act of ecstasy creates a lifetime of sorrows and failure.

And we have to teach that child to laugh at the cruel joke played on her. So she doesn't regret what we've done by bringing her here.

Fuck it.

I'm going to go outside and have fun with the people I love today. I'm free and nobody can stop me. This is the beginning of the beginning.

How To Avoid Death

My dad got depressed and would cry in the shopping store, cry at parent teacher conferences, cry while playing chess with me, cry at work, cry all the time.

He started a company in 1970 and it went public in, I think, 1984. The day it went public he was worth 5 million dollars on paper. About a year or so later he was worth zero and the company went bankrupt.

My parents bought a house but then couldn't pay for it so it was only half built.

All of the other houses seemed to be filled with happy people, children, cars, nice lawns, and then there was this one house in the middle that was half built and falling apart.

They bought it but they didn't buy it. Lawyers were involved.

Then the new company he worked for fired him and he got health insurance money to pay a portion of his salary. They fired him officially for "mental health reasons".

When I first made a lot of money I felt like I was going to avoid his curse.

I had money so I was completed as a person. That was it. I was done! I did it!

I bought a big house. I spent a lot of money. I bought other things. Lots of other things. I felt like I was immortal.

My dad would come by the new house while it was being built. He told the builder that we needed a power flush in each toilet.

We put the power flush in the guest toilet so he would always be able to use it and feel like he had made a contribution.

Then the same thing that happened to him, happened to me. I couldn't escape his curse. I was him.

He made money and lost all of it and became half of who he was. I made money and lost all of it and became a fraction of who I was.

He got divorced from his first wife. I got divorced.

When I was a kid I would work in his office in NYC at least once a month. I had acne so bad that he would take me to a dermatologist who would drain all the cysts on my face and then I'd be too embarrassed to go to school so I'd sit in his office and help the secretary run the copy machine.

Then at lunch he'd take me to the Carnegie Deli. Then he'd get the late afternoon New York Post and we'd go home and play either ping pong or chess until it was time for me to go to sleep.

I like to play games with my kids.

Therapists, family, friends, partners, all told me I wasn't like him. But I was broke and depressed and empty and I was afraid to sleep.

I knew I would wake up at three in the morning and I would feel lonely and scared and nothing at all could prevent it.

He had a fatal stroke when he was in the middle of an argument with someone who owed him money.

I'm afraid to repeat that mistake also.

Spending time with people you love and who inspire you is not about making money or having fun. It's a matter of life and death.

I got better at that part and it changed everything for me.

I removed the people who could kill me. And I surround myself with the people who give me life.

Maybe I broke the curse.

Today is my anniversary with Claudia. She laughed at me when I tred to explain to her I'm from another planet so there's no possible way her puny Earth mind could understand the love I feel for her.

Her dad is dead also.

And maybe one day in the distant future, if everything works out, I hope my children will be orphans as well.

HOW TO BE A TV STAR

I lied to get on TV. I wanted to go on Jim Cramer's show in 2003 and he asked me how much money I was managing. He said, "It has to be at least five million dollars else anyone just managing a few hundred thousand in family money can get on TV."

So I told him five million dollars.

I didn't want to go on TV at all. I was scared to death.

But I didn't want to go to Mississippi either.

I was supposed to go down to Mississippi to raise money for my business from the ex CFO of Worldcom and a family that killed more chickens per year than any other family in the country.

But I hadn't been on an airplane since having breakfast at the World Trade Center on September 11, 2001 and I didn't want to go on a plane.

Once Jim asked me to go on I couldn't stop shaking. I knew I was a fraud and I was finally going to prove it to everyone I went to high school with.

I assumed they would all be gathered at the same place, eating popcorn and laughing at me.

An hour before I went on, I met with Stephen Dubner, who

had yet to write Freakonomics. He had agreed to help me before I went on the air.

Before you go on a news show they send you the questions they want you to be ready for.

Stephen and I went to the studio and he asked me the questions over and over.

I kept repeating my answers trying to iron out all the "umms" and pauses and weird inflections. Trying to keep calm.

Going on TV is like going up to a strange girl in a bar and saying, "hey, do you think you like me?" and expecting a positive outcome.

Then they put you in this tiny room by yourself and there's a camera looking at you and there's a thing in your ear so you can hear the show.

Someone electronically whispers in your ear, "60 seconds". And then you begin to slightly pee in your pants.

On cue, you start talking out loud in an empty room to the thing in your ear with a cardboard picture of the NYC horizon behind you.

It's like a psychology experiment. "We're going to put you in a dark room, turn the lights down, and ask you a bunch of terrifying questions while we measure your sperm count! Hooozah!"

I asked the producer that the one question I did not want to answer was the one they sent about gold. Everything else I could answer.

They started off asking me about gold. Because all TV wants to do is completely crush your life. That's what's called "good TV".

Anyway, I answered it. Because as long as you open your mouth and English words come out, then everyone nods their head and says, "that's what I thought also".

You don't even have to say anything resembling a complete sentence. I think I answered, "Gold dollar money inflation nothing".

Oh, one piece of advice. No matter what people ask you on TV: bring it back to your "media message". So if someone asks about "Gold", just bring it back to, "it's all about the dollar". If someone asked me if Superman was secretly Jewish instead of from Krypton I could've said, "It really depends on how badly the Jews manipulated the Kryptonian dollar".

The entire time I was on TV was about 90 seconds. I had probably prepared 18 hours for those 90 seconds. Like most dates I had gone on in my 20s.

Afterwards two things happened.

My dad wrote me an email congratulating me. Since we were in a fight and I tend to avoid people I'm fighting, I didn't respond to him. Then he had a stroke and died.

Another thing happened.

I came home and my four year old daughter was having a religious awakening. I had just been on the TV, where God lives. And now I was standing in front of her, Christ risen.

She was more happy than I had ever seen her. She adored me more than she ever would again.

It's hard to be an authentic human being on television. And then you get addicted to the experience of being on it. The tiny box becomes a prison of ego.

On TV everyone pretends like they know the true price of everything.

I wasn't free until I finally appreciated that I knew the value of nothing.

How To Get Rich, The Push

Rob told me JB was dead. JB was my best friend growing up. We sat next to each other on the bus. After school we'd play ping pong or pinball or monopoly or ride bikes.

Every single day we did this for eight years. Then we drifted apart.

Rob said, The last time I spoke to him he sounded like a ghost.

It was like there was nothing there, Rob said.

I hadn't seen JB in 20 years.

He dropped out of college, Rob said, and never really had a job. His parents gave him money to live. He didn't want to do anything.

He changed his phone number every few weeks, Rob said. So he was hard to keep in touch with.

I didn't understand. Why did he change his number every few weeks?

He'd meet a girl, and then a few weeks later he'd get tired of her but not want to deal with it. He'd change his number so the girl couldn't reach him, Rob said. And he moved a lot.

He had no Facebook page, no internet presence, it was hard to track him down, Rob said.

And it's true. I had never found him on the Internet.

JB hurt his leg a few years ago, Rob said, and had no insurance because he never had a job. So got addicted to painkillers.

He was into the drug scene, Rob said.

So no job, drifting phone numbers, a hazy identity, drug, nerve damage, pain killers.

One day he never woke up, Rob said.

He was 39.

I don't feel sad about this. People die. I haven't seen him since we were 18 and on graduation day.

But I wonder about one thing Rob said.

"He was like a ghost the last time I spoke with him."

We know when the body and mind are giving up. We know when spirit is exhausted. When the emotions don't care.

He never had anything he wanted to do, Rob said.

Is that all it is? Do we just need something to do? Something that we want to scratch just a tiny bit so we continue one more day?

We don't have to save the world. Or invent warm ice. Or time travel. Or even have a passion or a purpose.

When I was dead broke and crying I wanted to die just so my kids could have my life insurance policy. What got me to get up and go again?

And then later, when it happened again. And then again.

Why didn't JB do that?

I call it "the push".

You're riding the bicycle up the hill all the time in life. Everything in life wants you to decay. To be subjugated. To be violated. To be tired. To become a ghost.

To roll back down the hill just when you thought you were

close to the top.

It's fucking tiring to live.

What can give us THE PUSH?

I don't know.

For me, today, it's just this chapter. Some days, it's to see my 11 year old smile. Sometimes, I just want to take a walk. Or help Claudia. Or do something fun and creative.

What's your PUSH today?

A little bit, every day, compounds.

A little push today turns into a big life tomorrow.

My one requirement: I have to give something. I have to enjoy it.

Else, it's too draining. It's a shit stain. I slip back on the hill.

A deep breath. You can do it, I tell myself. One more turn of the pedals. THE PUSH! Get over the hill!

I want to live.

I Want To Live

When we learned square dancing in seventh grade the pregnant girl (but nobody knew it yet) told all her friends "it's ok if you don't touch him", meaning me. So no girl would touch me.

Holding our hands in the air and moving to the music. The girls pretending like their hands were holding mine. But we were just miming it. I didn't mind. I was afraid to upset them if they touched me.

My pimples were so big I had to practically wear condoms on them to avoid the pus going down my face like tears.

Junior High was a nightmare. I went to that little Jewish elementary school. Then suddenly five elementary schools piled into the junior high... Linwood.

"Holy fuck," I remember Jonathan said as we pulled into the school parking lot for the first time. Everyone from our clean suburban block was horrified.

We couldn't believe what these creatures looked like. I mean, some of them had beards. Some of them were smoking. They were wearing plaid and jeans and they were all eight feet tall.

Jews at that age are about 5 feet, on the way to a solid 5'9". And that's about it.

When Jews hated each other we would say stuff like, "you stupid fuck!" and and then cry.

58

When these kids hated us they would punch us until there was blood, put one foot on our heads and spit chewing tobacco on our eyes.

These kids could already crush our dads and make our dads kiss each against their wills. It wasn't any good anymore to say, "My dad is a VP at Macy's and he will KICK YOUR ASS!" That didn't work anymore.

I had never really been punched before. Now it became a habit. And then people would stand around and laugh.

It's ok. I don't know.

And now my daughter is in eighth grade. When the hell did that happen? How did you get so old, my little cutie?

Are you punching anyone? Or is anyone punching you?

I never told my parents either.

Is anyone trying to kiss you? I hope not. That's disgusting!

I hope you are nicer to people than people were to me.

I hope if there's someone who everyone picks on, then maybe you can be friends with them.

There were other kids like me. Other kids nobody was friends with. But I couldn't be friends with them. It didn't work like that. It wasn't like "The Super Fraternity of Cool People Nobody was Friends With". We all thought we were better than the people just like us.

I had one friend. And now I can't even find him on Facebook. He was suicidal all the time. Only eight years later he told me he was suicidal because he realized he was gay. Then his dad died of AIDs. And now he's missing.

I had to hold in my pee from 8am to 5pm every day. I couldn't go to the bathroom in school or I would be killed. Or peed on while people laughed.

Lesson number one in How To Be Rich: Always know that Junior High doesn't last forever.

HOW TO BE THE KING
OF THE WORLD

I can totally dominate my 11 year old daughter in tennis. I kick her ass basically.

Like, if she hits an easy shot, I can slam it back to the other side of the court and with her small legs there's no way she can run to catch the ball.

That's the way I roll. I destroy the dreams of 11-year-old girls.

Here's the problem: I get tired. After about eight minutes I'm too exhausted to play anymore.

She's like, "Daddy, what's wrong?" But after all the strenuous work of slamming shots, dominating her with my topspin, running the net, lobbing, serving, etc I need a break.

My breath can't be caught and for some reason I'm spitting gray gunk onto the ground.

We say kids have a lot of energy. Do they have a battery? Is it fully charged? Do they have more electronic chemicals or something? How does it work?

I'm older and I'm better at everything. And I know everything because I'm the father.

I can see her or my other daughter and I can see the life around them. I'm not talking about "auras". I don't know what that is. But just LIFE. They have it.

They ooze it. They spray it everywhere. And it comes out smart and it comes out stupid. It doesn't matter. They can waste it at that age. They have enough to spare.

I have to bottle mine. Use it appropriately.

In Jimmy Connors autobiography he talks about how he started breaking down when he was #1 in the world in tennis. The new guns (John McEnroe) were coming up and beating him. He couldn't hit #1 anymore. His bones were tired.

He was 29 years old.

Ok, that's ok. That's why I like chess and not tennis.

So I took a look at a list of the top 100 chessplayers in the world. They must be a bunch of old men.

#1, Magnus Carlsen, was born the year after I graduated college. I had to scroll down to #65 to find someone who was older than me. Julio Zuniga. Three months older than me.

I was at a conference last week of entrepreneurs. There were 15 speakers. I was one of them. Tim Ferriss was another. Marc Ecko was another. Lots of smart people. I was the oldest speaker.

But then I realized: out of the 110 people in the audience, I was older than all of them as well.

Where is everyone? Did they put the 45 year olds in a concentration camp? Is that even appropriate to say? Did they put the 45 year old Jews in a concentration camp?

Did I miss the exit on the ramp and end up in the under-45 year old world?

I feel better than when I was 20. And I know more about

things. A lot more.

I could write a book with what I know!

I know that when a spouse starts telling me her problems, I need to LISTEN and not SOLVE her problems.

I know that if someone says, "I have a great opportunity for you", then he is trying to send fuckness in my direction.

I create my opportunities. In my entire life nobody has ever magically given me one.

The only magic I believe in is when I cast the spells. I have 45 years worth of spells to cast.

I know at 45 that if I'm not happy "here" then there's even less chance I will be happy "there", in whatever daydream "there" exists.

But what the hell, every day is a battle: with depression, with health, with money worries (no matter how much you have, or how little), with love, with kids, with the institutions that always try to imprison us and scare us, with the arguments that always try to engage us.

One of my best friends for 20 years is no longer speaking to me. He brought up a web post I wrote two years ago that angered him. It was my anti-war post.

"Are you kidding?" I asked. I was so shocked. But he didn't respond. He's no longer speaking to me. Some years I lose friends. Some years I make friends. What's the point of dwelling on it?

And I know if I let anything bother me, if I don't truly appreciate the things in my life, if I don't cherish the moment, and take care of my body and mind and emotions and spirit, then I can start to age.

We don't just have a physical body. We have emotional, mental, and spiritual ones also. They all age. They all need to be taken care of and exercised and fed nourishing food.

Energy changes. I still have the energy of my youth. But it's spread now through my other bodies.

Now I have to go and crush the hopes and dreams out of my 11 year old on the tennis court. Someone has to teach her the harsh realities of life.

And yes, then I will feel like the king of the world.

For about eight minutes. Until she is standing over me, laughing, with her tennis racquet raised in victory.

THERE'S NO PAINLESS WAY TO KILL YOURSELF

I gave my 11 year old daughter important advice the other day: there's no painless way to kill yourself.

"What about with a gun?" she said.

I told her about a friend of mine who shot himself in the mouth. He put the gun in his mouth and pointed upwards towards the brain.

He missed.

He shot off half his face, he went blind in one eye, and he is now in a wheelchair.

If you type in "I Want to Die" into google, my website is the first result.

My first business I sold for $15 million. We built websites for entertainment companies. Bad Boy Records, Miramax, Time Warner, HBO, Sony, Disney, Loud Records, Interscope, on and on. Oh, and Con Edison.

Mobb Deep would hang out in my office. Trent Reznor from Nine Inch Nails would stop by. RZA from the Wu-Tang Clan would want to play chess. We even made a website for a brothel in Nevada.

Then I saw that kids in junior high school were learning HTML. So I sold the business.

I bought an apartment for millions. I rebuilt it. Feng Shui! I bought art. I played a lot of poker. I began investing in companies. A million here. A few hundred thousand there.

Then I started more companies. Then I bought more things. Then I became an addict. The worst kind of addict.

From June 2000 until September, 2001 I probably lost $1 million a month.

I couldn't stop. I wanted to get back up to the peak.

I wanted to be loved. I wanted to have $100 million so people would love me.

Writing this now I even feel like slitting my wrists and stomach. I have 2 kids.

I felt like I was going to die. That zero equals death. I couldn't believe how stupid I had been.

I lost all my friends. Nobody returned calls. I would go to the ATM machine – from $15 million to $143 left.

There were no jobs, There was nothing.

One weekend when I had $0 left in my bank account I called my parents to borrow money but they said "no". "College was enough," they told me, even though I had ended up paying for every dime of college. That was the last time I spoke to my dad, who had a stroke six months later.

I tried meditation to calm down but it didn't work. I never slept. I lost 30 lbs. I'm 5'9". I went from 160 to 130. I couldn't talk to anyone. I couldn't move. I stopped having ideas. I cried every day.

There was never a moment when I didn't feel sick. I had let my kids down. I would die and they would never remember me.

We moved 80 miles north of NYC with the tiny bit of money

we took out of our apartment after being forced to sell at a million dollar loss.

I couldn't leave the house for three months. I was depressed. I gained back all my weight and then another 30 lbs.

Finally I had to either die or feed my family. I was forced to choose myself.

* I started to exercise every day. I started to eat better. One item for breakfast. A healthy lunch. Tiny dinner. No snacks.
* I started to sleep 9 hours a day.
* I started to only be around people who loved and supported me. I broke off all ties with anyone who I felt bad to be around.
* I wrote down ideas every day of articles I could write and about businesses I could start. Bit by bit I started to get paid to write. If you don't exercise the idea muscle it atrophies.
* I decided I wanted to help people every day and be honest every day. I was grateful for my daughters. I was grateful for what I had. I didn't fight reality or regret. This was my reality and I had to make the best of it.
* Every day I came up with ideas for new businesses. I had a waiter's pad. I would go to a cafe at 6 in the morning with about 4 books and read for an hour or two and then start writing down ideas for new businesses, articles, etc.
* I started a hedge fund. I started a fund of hedge funds. I started a newsletter. I did deals. I made introductions every day, expanding my brand new network from scratch. At least 5 introductions a day.
* I got involved in a mental health company I sold for $41mm.
* I started a website, Stockpickr! Which got millions of unique users. I found advertising for it. I sold it to thestreet.com
* I had made millions again from scratch.

Then I stopped using the fundamental techniques I described above. Every time I've lost money it's because I squandered my physical, emotional, mental, and spiritual health.

I was really bad. I did everything you should not do. I was like an addict. Picture the worst abuses. That was me. Again.

And then I lost it all again. Everything. Agh!

I had to start over. I couldn't even believe I had to start from scratch again.

Every day without fail I focus on physical, emotional, mental, and spiritual health. And it's worked. I hope. I hope I don't squander again.

People say it's not about the end, it's about the journey.

This is total BS.

It's not about the journey and it never was.

It's about right now.

Right now is the only place you'll ever be. Choose yourself not to waste it.

THE DAY I STOPPED A TEN MILLION DOLLAR ROBBERY

I stopped a ten million dollar robbery last week.

For various reasons, including Claudia is slightly worried I could get killed, I am changing all of the names. All of the other details are intact.

A few weeks ago, a guy claiming to be related to Middle Eastern royalty, (call him "M"), had a representative (a friend of a friend of a friend) call me and ask me if I knew anyone who would lend M ten million dollars.

"He has collateral," the rep said: "$25 million in restricted shares of [well known private Internet company]."

So I called a fund I used to be an investor in. They were interested and made an offer. Call the fund manager, "Bill".

Bill said, "We'll lend $10 million IF we get the full $25 million on any default." Here were the other terms Bill said.

- 15% interest, paid quarterly
- The full loan is due back in two years
- $600,000 fee paid to Bill up front.

- Bill wanted 25% of all the upside on the full $25 million in shares for the next ten years.

I had never seen a term in a loan like that last one but I give Bill credit. Why not ask for it? In a negotiation it never hurts to ask for anything.

M said, "yes". He needed the money fast for some real estate he wanted to buy.

Bill began his due diligence. M sent a fax picture of the shares. His lawyers sent over all the contracts M had signed to get those shares. M even wired $15,000 to Bill to pay for Bill's legal fees. M wanted no hurdles to getting the deal done. Lawyers on both sides were busy every day all day, working out the details.

Bill said to M: I need permission from the internet company that I would be the potential shareholder if you default.

It took a day but M sent over a letter. It was written on the Internet company's letterhead, signed by the company's "Director of Investor Relations" giving Bill permission to control the shares in a default and "call me at XYZ phone number if you have any questions."

By coincidence, I knew the Director of Investor Relations but hadn't spoken to him in a year or so.

Finally, last Friday, Bill calls me in the morning. He was about to wire ten million dollars to M.

"I don't know," Bill said, "I have to tell you, James, something seems funny."

"What?"

"The letter from the head of investor relations at the company. It almost seemed too simple. Why didn't he throw in a line indemnifying the company?"

"I don't know," I said. I had no clue. "Is that standard?"

"I don't know either," Bill said and he sort of drifted, "I just don't know. But something makes me feel funny."

"I have an idea," I said, "I know the guy who wrote that letter. I'll write to him and ask him if he wrote that letter. This way he independently verifies."

Bill said, "ok, do it." So I did.

I didn't hear back. Bill called again two hours later.

Bill said, "Look, let's call up the number on this letter. You stay quiet."

So Bill called and someone picked up and said he was "X", the head of investor relations for this company. I've spoken to X a few times before. The voice did not sound like X but it had been awhile.

Bill and X started talking about the letter. Then Bill said, "hey, by the way, I have your friend, James Altucher on the line to say Hi."

CLICK.

Dial tone.

"We got disconnected," I said.

Bill started laughing.

"JAMES!" he said.

"What?"

"This is a total fraud! That was a fake phone number. That guy was an actor! Do you think it was an accident we got disconnected the second I said you were on the phone?"

I felt like an idiot.

"I don't understand. Why would they go through all of that?"

Bill said, "Holy shit, I almost wired $10 million. That's why they did it!"

"I don't get any of this," I said. I was in denial. I had never seen a $10 million robbery in action.

Then X, the ACTUAL head of investor relations at the

company, wrote back to me. He said, "Stop by for coffee next time you are in SF. Meanwhile, I will contact your friend Bill about this letter you sent me." Nothing else.

I called Bill.

"Yeah, X is all up in my grill about where I got this letter supposedly signed by him. He had never signed it. He wanted to know who was involved, etc. The shares were forged. That guy we called was fake. The contracts were forged. Signatures were forged. This is a total fraud. Authorities are being notified. It's all bad."

Meanwhile, M, and his lawyers, had all disappeared at this point. No more contact. Nobody picking up their phones according to Bill.

"Ugh," I said. I felt sick. "I'm sorry I even introduced you to these guys."

Bill said, "Don't worry. We're in the business of looking at all opportunities. You helped figure this out. Without you I prob- ably would've wired. But I'm glad I had a hunch."

So I have to give Bill credit again. I've ignored my hunches many times and paid the price. When your body whispers to you, you have to listen.

There's a lot of bad people in the world. All they want to do is destroy and vanish. They roam the world like pirates.

A network of lawyers, escrows, fake shares, bank accounts, bogus corporations and banks, all set up to hide them in the shadows. A network of relationships and lies. The dark side of the force.

Sometimes they are fake royalty. Sometimes they are your neighbors. Your friend. Your family. Your whatever.

Sometimes the fraud is your bank account. Sometimes your heart.

I had to go. I went to my daughter's high school play. I sat outside in the parking lot of the school for a few minutes. I was shaking. We had spoken to Evil on the phone.

I went into the school. I hate plays but I liked watching my daughter on stage.

Then I wrote this post. "Maybe don't publish it," Claudia said. "It could be dangerous".

I want life to be simple and good. I don't want my head to hurt. I don't want to deal with bad people.

Sometimes you just have to take a deep breath and say "thank you" without understanding why.

"Thank you".

Sometimes people ask me what I do for a living.

I solve crimes.

WITH ALL DUE RESPECT

I wanted ten million from him. I was raising money for a fund. He allocated money for a large fund of hedge funds. He visited my office. I visited his office in Seattle. Everything was going well.

He then called me a few days before he was to send over the ten million, "the shit hit the fan," he said. Everything in my life fell apart when he said that. An extra $10mm in the fund meant about an extra $100k in an income for me give or take. And he potentially could've been good in the long run for another $50 million for my fund. I knew that meant I wasn't getting the money. "What happened?"

One of the funds he invested in turned out to be a Ponzi scheme. All the money was gone. "Nobody will trust us again," he said. He was afraid he was going to go out of business. Lose his job. All fund allocations were shut down. No money was coming. But I still wanted the money.

I called him every other day. He was very depressed. "How could we have caught them?" he said. He kept second-guessing himself. "This is very very bad." He thought his career was over. I tried to help in various ways. I introduced him to reporters so he could get his story out. I told him that his career didn't amount to one little thing. That this happened in the hedge fund industry all the time. In fact, as I write this, I personally think about 90% of hedge funds are frauds.

So instead of talking about the fund, we talked about what he was going through. The depression he was experiencing. I barely knew him but we talked several times a week. About everything: the business, his family, the psychology of frauds, the psychology of getting through periods like this. Eventually, months and months later, the dust settled. He was able to allocate money again. He put $10 million in my fund. Later he put even more money in.

Then in 2006 I decided to shut down the fund. We were up for everyone but I didn't like the strategy we had anymore. The strategy was getting too crowded and I thought in the long run it would collapse. I was eventually right but at the time it didn't seem like that would happen. In any case, we sent back everyone's money. I don't like to gamble with anyone's money. Even if it meant short-term loss of income for me.

And about a year later I called him again with a new idea I had. "So you're raising a new fund," he said.

"Yes". I told him what the strategy was.

"With all due respect," he said, his voice cold and steel-like, "why should I trust you after you shut down the last fund?"

I was shocked. I felt I had been there with him in the trenches. Now…this. I felt horrible for a second. Like I wasn't worth anything. Like any hope I had for a career in the hedge fund business was over. I said, "I guess you can't." And I shut down the phone and checked my records. He had definitely made money with me on the last fund. I never spoke to him again.

I didn't understand how he could be such a jerk when I had tried to be kind to him when he was down. "With all due respect" kept going through my head. Five years later I still hear it. I heard it this morning. I heard it while I was reading. "With all due respect." Motherfucker. His ability to wield power over me. His technique to make me feel bad worked. I felt bad. I still do when I keep myself trapped in the memory, like a soap bubble that never fully pops as it goes from all colors to a soapy brown, to an invisible black that's still hanging on, filled with air it won't let escape.

This doesn't mean you shouldn't be kind to people when they need your help. And it doesn't mean you shouldn't be disappointed when things don't go the way you expect. Nothing ever really does. And it doesn't mean you shouldn't trust people or love them or whatever. Because they are just going through their own things and you have no idea what's really going on inside their heads. We all have problems.

At that time, four years ago, I had no idea what his rejection of me would mean. It just felt bad. There's a saying in AA, "it's your best thinking that got you here." But that's not quite true. It's not only my best thinking. It's everyone else's best thinking. It all got me here. And I sincerely trust that the best thinking of the world got me to where I am right now, writing you. Enjoying the sun rise. Enjoying a coffee.

Who would ever think the words, "with all due respect" would turn out so wonderfully. And every day the best thinking will carry me through the day if I let it, don't fight it, don't argue with it, don't regret it, don't fear it. Every day I try and surround myself only with "the best thinking". I get a little better at it each day.

I don't know what ever happened to that hedge fund manager. He might be a big success. He might be out of business. He might even be dead. I sincerely thank him for his "due respect". I am here. I am still alive.

THREE CARD MONTE
FOR YOUR SOUL

I couldn't believe I was about to make 50 dollars. I was only 12 years old. Robert and I were standing on the corner of 45th and Broadway, right near Times Square. The guy had his cardboard table with three card son it. "Where's the Queen?" "Where's the Queen?" He was flipping the cards back and forth, every now and then lifting one up to show us the queen. One girl said, "I know where it is!" and she threw down $5 and he lifted up the card and it was a Jack. "Damn!" she said. Another guy pointed to a card, "its that one." The guy doing the cards said, "that's right," and he turned over the queen, "but you didn't bet." The guy who pointed turned to me and said, "Ugh, I could've won twenty dollars."

He did it again. It looked so obvious to me. And of course, I thought, I was smarter than everyone here. I could see the Queen right through the cards as if I had X-ray vision. The guy who picked the right card the first time pointed again. "10 will get you thirty" the card table guy said. The guy picking the card threw down a $10. The card was turned over. The Queen! He got his $30. Of course it was that card, I thought. This is so easy!

One guy in a suit walked by Robert and me and whispered, "Get away. It's a scam." But what did he know? He just got there. He was just passing by. He didn't see the Queen like I did.

Next one. The cards flipping back and forth. "$20 will get you $50!" The guy said. Everyone around the table was encouraging me. "Pick a card," said the first woman. Robert and I were visiting his dad's office a few blocks away when we decided to take a walk past the arcades in Broadway. Then we ran into this table. Then I wanted to make money. $50 meant I would be able to take a cab to school maybe. So people on the bus wouldn't bully me anymore. Heck, maybe I'd even take a limo. All the girls would like that.

"I don't know," Robert said. "That guy said it was a scam."

"20 will get you $80! Where's the card, young man!" I was sure I knew. I pointed to one of the three face-down cards. "Where's the 20?" the guy said, "I have to see the 20!"

I didn't have $20. I asked Robert. His dad was a stockbroker. I was sure he had $20. "Just show the $20," I said to Robert, "it's definitely that card to the right."

"I don't have a $20," Robert said.

"Ok," the guy said, "your watch will get you $80. All you have to do is hold up your watch and point to the card."

Robert took off his watch. It was a nice watch. When I think back on it now I think it was a gold watch but that's probably not true. I just know it was a nice watch. Robert had nice everything. He always had cashmere sweaters. A sweater for every day of the month. The guy held out $80. "I'll hold everything," he said, "and you pick and get everything back."

He took the watch and had his $80 in his hand. I pointed to what I was sure was the right card. I was following every movement of that card. The guy flipped the card over and it was...a Jack. "Ooohhh," everyone in the crowd said.

Robert said, "I knew it." I said, "I'm sorry". The girl who we first saw playing said, "Police coming!" and the guy folded up the table, everyone around us disappeared, the guy disappeared, the girl disappeared, Robert's watch disappeared, my future wealth disappeared, my limo picking me up and taking me to school disappeared. Robert and I were standing there by ourselves, a ghost-like white bracelet carved into his skin where his watch had been. "Shit," he said. "My dad is going to kill me."

He was crying on the elevator when we went upstairs. His dad got worried right away. "What's wrong?" he said. Robert told the whole story. I would not have told the whole story. I would've made something up. But Robert said everything. His dad hit Robert on the back. "You stupid shit!" Robert slouched down and when he straightened up his dad hit him again, "You are one dumb fuck!" Robert was crying. We didn't talk again on the ride back and they dropped me off at home. My parents asked me if I had a fun time in the city. "It was ok," I said, and went into my room. Star Trek was about to come on.

3 card monte has been around since the 1500s. The word monte comes from a legit card game played in Mexico in the 1800s and when the scam made it's way into the US via Louisiana in the 1830s it took that name to give it a veneer of legitimacy. Ever since then, the guy behind the card table has been using sleight of hand, shills who would pretend to play, a crowd egging on the victim, and every other classic technique in the book to make money. Millions have been made. As far as I know, NOBODY running the con has ever lost money.

And why does it work? Because of illusion. Not just the sleight of hand, the illusion of quickly replacing one card with another without anyone noticing, or the legitimacy of the name, or the fact that's it's just cards. But the illusion created by the crowd, the excitement that builds up until the only way it can relieve some of the pressure is if YOU pick the card, the climax of the illusion, when everything is downhill after that. The excitement is all an illusion. The other people betting are all illusion. The crowd that surrounds you so you can no longer back out and you are slowly pushed closer and closer to the table is all an illusion. The police is an illusion so they can quickly abscond with your money and find another mark. The illusion exists on at least five different levels. And always it ends with the victim alone, minus his money, and about to be punished in some way, either by his own regrets, or the fist of a father.

And then we look around Times Square and we are bombarded with the illusions that then carry us through the rest of our lives. All life is a three card monte. The commercial images. The shows on TV or in the news ("Greece worries plunge markets!" If I hear that one more time well, I'm going to do nothing, but I'm sure I'm going to hear it at least 100 more times). The pressures of our friends, peers, parents, colleagues. The pressure to OWN a home ("ROOTS!"), go to college ("you won't get a job otherwise!"), the need for success and ambition, the need for $100 million to push off mortality, the need for us to fight every four years ("it's either US or THEM who will run or ruin the country" , turning our friends and neighbors from full-blooded humans into plastic figurines who will either ruin or save us depending on who is elected).

Just like in 3 card monte, the key is to just stand back and observe the illusion. You can't stop the illusion. But you don't have to put up your money. You can just observe. You learn to observe by every day checking the "X" on some small, incremental self improvement physically, emotionally (be around positive people), mentally (be an idea machine) and spiritually (be grateful for the world we are in this moment). Then, as an observer, you can marvel at the beauty of the sleight of hand. The psychology that turns three cards on a cardboard box into MAGIC. How beautiful that is. Marvel at the way people manipulate the mark. Laugh in delight at the way everyone disappears when imaginary police are spotted. It's all-beautiful. It's all entertainment.

Everything is theater. You are either an actor in the theater (and in almost every case, you are "the mark" 99% of the time) or you are in the audience. Being in the audience is fun. You can watch the illusion unfold in everything around you. You can admire the production quality. You can laugh at the things you find funny. The more illusions you train yourself to observe, the more fun you will have. Spot the illusion in everything. Appreciate the art of it. Appreciate the magic created by all the humans around us as they try to get us into their imaginary worlds and vision.

And once the show is over, the entertainers exit stage left. The curtain comes down. You can leave. The sun is outside and it's time for you to enjoy it.

IMAGINARY LETTER FROM MY TEENAGE DAUGHTER TO ME

Dear Dad,

I'm sorry I walked in the house the other day, didn't say "hi", and just walked into my room and locked the door. I have these hormones that are being triggered that are encouraging me to explore the world and that means I'm feeling an irrational need to not interact with the people I interacted with for the first thirteen years of my life. I hope you understand.

I'm also sorry I yelled at you when you were late taking me to dance classes. I know I've been late for just about every other event in my life and you've always had to wait for me in the car, which is particularly worrisome since you're always talking about how you don't have a driver's license but nevertheless… when I need to go to things I need you to be ready in advance even though I'm always late.

And I apologize for always singing even though you asked me to please stop when you were writing. I don't really know what you are writing over there anyway. Does it make money?

And I need to sing because I want to get the lead part in lots of plays. I hope you aren't writing about me, by the way. If you are, please take it down. My friends might see and think I'm weird for having such a weird father.

Dad, also, you and Mollie took a walk by the river the other day. I know you really wanted me to join you. But I did have math homework to do even though, up to that moment, I had not yet touched my math homework that weekend. But it was really important. And, to be honest, there was a slight chance I would run into people I knew if I went on a walk with you and Mollie. This is not to say I don't want to be seen with you. I would never say that. But lets just say I didn't want to run into people I knew while I was out walking with you.

As for food: anything you make me I will not eat. But if you don't make me food I will not eat anything. I know this seems like a contradiction. Sometimes the universe works that way. It might be just best if we order pizza from now on. But when you asked me to do the actual ordering the other day I was really tired and I fell asleep instantly and I probably never heard you ask me. I'm glad I woke up before the pizza arrived. It was really delicious. Can you get pepperonis next time, though?

On my birthday I would like a laptop. All of the other kids have one. And no, there is no way for you to confirm that. But we have a lot of homework now that requires laptops. Ugh, I can picture you asking me "what homework?" I don't know! Nothing! But we do get a lot of homework that will be easier to do with a laptop. I promise I won't take it into my bedroom. But sometimes I need quiet. And I like the Macbook Air because all Apple products are cooler than those other laptops. They are clunky or something.

Also, just so you know: I don't know how to use a dishwasher, a toaster, a laundry machine, a microwave oven, the regular oven, and I'm not really sure how to make my bed. Some of these items are too hard for me to reach. And a lot of times an important new TV show is on ("Victorious"!) so I can't take out the garbage at the same time. I can do it later, though? But then I get tired. I've needed a lot of sleep lately and I don't want to get sick.

Finally, Daddy, when you keep bringing up that it was just a few years ago I was so happy to see you, blah blah, and that I wasn't as popular, blah blah, and I was a little more pudgier, etc etc I don't really know what you mean. That was so long ago and you keep saying just focus on living life now. I love you, Daddy, and so I'm going to take your advice.

Bye!

GIRL WITH THE NAME THAT WAS A CURSE

I only met a girl once in a bar that I actually fell hard for. It was the bar at El Quijote, which was a restaurant attached to The Chelsea Hotel. The restaurant itself is great and underappreciated by the foodies who love to go the latest momofukos or wherever the latest hip restaurants are. All of the waiters have been working there forever, and in a weird sort of inbreeding math that I could never figure out, all of the parents of the waiters and staff had at some point worked there. I would go there when I was sick with the flu and could barely move and I would order the hottest soup possible to warm me up. I would also sit at the bar at night and read and drink until I practically fell asleep at the bar. The door in the back went straight into the elevators at the Chelsea and within minutes I could be asleep in my bed.

She was with somebody else but it seemed like they barely knew each other and he was going back and forth between her and some other party at the other end of the restaurant. We began to talk and in one of those odd eclipses of nature that seem to happen once or twice in a lifetime, I guessed her last name right there at the bar like I was a psychic. She said, "you could never guess my name". She looked Jewish and I thought of a Jewish-sounding name that had a curse embedded in it. "That's it!" she said. "How did you guess that?"

Actually, I lied a little bit. I met someone else there about eight months before the girl above. It was exactly 15 years ago today, Christmas Eve. I was seeing someone who had kicked me out of her apartment after a horribly personal argument where she ended up crying and I had narrowly avoided a black eye. There was a girl at the bar who I had seen many times before. She lived in the Hotel as well. She had short blonde hair and would often stand at the bar instead of sitting, even if the bar was empty. This one night, perhaps because it was Christmas Eve and the world shuts down for a little bit, I had nothing at all to lose so started talking to her. Somehow it got around in conversation to the fact that she couldn't sit down. "After a day of my work, you'd understand. I can't sit." She told me of what happened to her earlier in that work day. A client came over to her apartment with a bag of groceries. Fruits, whip cream, chocolate, I don't know. Everything that people can eat. She took off her clothes and he poured the food over every inch of her body while she was standing up. Then he took a photograph of her and turned away from her while looking at the photograph.

When you hear someone, almost a complete stranger, telling you a story like this, what do you say? Do you say, yeah I had a weird day at work also. I just sit there. I wanted to hear more but there's nothing really to say.

After he was done, she told me, she wanted him out as quickly as possible But she gave him a vacuum cleaner and told him to clean up while she showered. Which he did. "My whole room was spotless," she said. "It was cleaner than before he got there. And he gave a good tip. Cheers."

It was Christmas Eve but for whatever reason, the bar was starting to fill up. "Wait a second," said the guy next to me as if he'd been participating in our conversation all along, "did you say you did that for money?" This guy was fascinated. "You mean," he said, "I can pay you right now and within ten minutes I could be having a sexual experience." He was clinical. Like a scientist. At that point I was thinking about the fight I had earlier with my girlfriend at the time. I wish I could tell you what we were fighting about but despite what I tend to reveal here, this one was far too persona l and sitting there listening to these two negotiate made me both embarrassed and melancholy. I paid the bill and left. The other guy took my seat.

But back to the first girl. The girl with the last name that had a curse in it. I called her the next day after I met her. "Oh every-one has a web development company," she told me, clearly not interested in the Internet or anything I was doing with it. Who needed the Internet? For a short time she ended up working for me on and off. During one of those times I tried to kiss her but it was one of those kisses where clearly the other person was not interested. I remember calling her on Valentine's Day but she said she'd call me back and she never did.

I've had lots of things happen to me at El Quijote over 15 years. If I were to count the number of stories that were worth telling it would easily be over thirty or forty. Some bad, some good. Two years ago, I met a girl there that was the first date I went on after getting separated from my wife. She told me her job was to keep track of the various terrorists based in New York City that were allowed to run free. She worked in some branch of the New York Police Department but "I'm not a cop." Her group would tap phones, follow the people, and do what-ever it took to see if something was going on. "Everyone who is still left in Guantanamo Bay is a hard-core terrorist," she said. "If Obama releases them they will all commit future acts of terrorism." I wanted her to tell me more stories. Secrets. "I work right near here," she said, but wasn't allowed to tell me where, not even what block. My only thought then was that if we ever had a relationship I would never be able to find her during the day.

If you ever go there, order the skirt steak. Or any of the rice dishes. The place has red checkered tablecloths, like something old-fashioned and certainly uncool. The first time I went there I was so pleased at the find. But sometimes when you have such experiences in a place it might be best not to go back there anymore. The karma is too thick and you can end up dying from love.

PROSTITUTES, DRUGS, HBO, AND THE BEST JOB I EVER HAD

The best job I ever had was interviewing prostitutes, junkies, homeless kids, and other random creatures at three in the morning. I did it for about two and a half years. People who knew me then ask me now, "how did you go from interviewing drug dealers to doing stuff with stocks?" Isn't it the same thing? The job started because HBO didn't have a website or an intranet. I was constantly on the verge of getting fired because I wasn't interested in the random database stuff they wanted from me. So one weekend I put the HBO cafeteria menu on an intranet I set up, using a server I set up on my computer. Then I put their employee database on there, then their movie database, and so on. Until they had an intranet and everyone started using it. I forgot to ask for permission. Comedy Central called me and asked me if I could help do the same thing for them

So I went up there and they said they were willing to pay me as a consultant. Maybe I had a small crush on the IT woman there who asked me. But I might've had a crush on everyone back then. I told her I would only do it they gave me the time slot on Comedy Central from 3 to 4 in the morning to do whatever I wanted. I wanted to have my own talk show. A few days later she called me and said she asked her boss or her boss's boss and he said no. They sell that time slot for infomercials. So I then approached HBO and said, "you guys are great at doing original TV shows, how about let me do an original web show." So that's how I did "III:am" for 2.5 years. Every Tuesday night I would go out at three in the morning and interview whoever I could find.

Why a Tuesday night? Because anyone could be out on a Saturday night at 3 in the morning. Saturday nights at three in the morning are boring. But if YOU were out and about at 3 in the morning on a Tuesday night, then there's a reason. You probably don't work a regular nine to five job. You probably don't do a regular anything. You're out at three in the morning on a Tuesday night either causing trouble or avoiding it.

I turned over every rock in the city for two years. For instance, there's a bus that goes back and forth from Queens to Rikers Island. It runs all night long because if someone can get bailed out, they get out of jail right then. The bus stop had the constant buzz of misfortune. There were construction workers who would secretly whisper to me that they were cops. There were the teenage prostitutes who were waiting for boyfriends or clients to get out of jail. There were the drug dealers and pimps ready to sell whatever to whoever. And in the middle of it all were the nervous moms and sisters getting ready to get on the bus to go bail out their kids and brothers. Once someone got on that bus I never saw them again.

Other Tuesdays I'd go over to the east side of Manhattan. Everything was happening there. How many times did I fall in love? I can't even begin to say. Homeless girls in dreadlocks living in the shanty town on the other side of FDR across from the housing projects on Avenue D. A girl with a stutter carrying a monkey in a cage. Everyone trying to belt out their story and be heard in the middle of the night because the shackles that shut them up during the day were sound asleep. For two years I interviewed hundreds of people, taking their pictures, transcribing the tapes, and putting four interviews a week up on the HBO website (with the help of a great crew of people at HBO. I still miss Trish). Everyone had to sign a release form and put their phone numbers, which for awhile was the only way I would get a date or two when someone caught my eye and I'd call them the day after, trying to read their number off of the crumpled release form.

It was a different world at three in the morning. The same locations, but different rules, different customs, different cultures. There was the working world (people working in clubs, all night diners, even the NY times workers putting the final touches on all the news that was fit to print), and then there were the forgotten outcasts from that world: homeless, jobless, addicted, disabled. Couples arguing in the middle of the street, johns, pimps, prostitutes, lonely people looking to add excitement to their lives. The sadder and more twisted a story was, the more beautiful to me. I would get home at five in the morning (after treating my crew to breakfast at the all-night Empire Diner) and I would lie awake, buzzed for hours until falling asleep for a half hour here and there.

THE THINGS I LEARNED:

- All the rules we think of as normal society are all manufactured. There's no such thing as normal.
- There's a 3AM religion: there are too many sides of life to count. Each with its own special despair and story. Each with its own way of escaping the chains that bind us to the day. The sadness was unbearable but only then do you see God in their eyes looking back.

LIVE SEX, CHESS, AND SHAME

Ylon called me, "You have to come to this party. It's right around the corner from your apartment! There's live sex performances in one room and a chess tournament with all the top grandmasters in another room." I thought he was lying to me. I had been asleep. I got some clothes on and went downstairs.

The party was being thrown by pseudo.com. The party was running 24 hours a day from December, 1999 through January 2000. They filed for bankruptcy 9 months later in September, 2000. Sometime in January the investors of the company came and shut down the party. But that was a million years later. I met Ylon outside around midnight and we went into the party. There was crazy in the air. I wanted to drink it up. I was thirsty in a desert. I ran into Josh Harris, the CEO of pseudo in the middle of the party and I said hi but he had no idea who I was. We had met several times before. He was distracted by the fifty girls around him.

Ylon said, "I'm trying to get Josh to do a show about me playing chess around the world and the adventures I get into." That's a great idea, I said. Anything was possible. Chess, sex, shows, money, whatever. Whatever you want, man, as I pushed through the people to figure it all out.

The live sex performance room was having an issue. Any couple could get into a "pod" and just start having sex. There were video cameras in the room streaming it live onto the Internet. There were no doors on the pods so people could stand there and watch. The problem was that, as it was then explained to me, if you're a guy and not a professional porn actor, it's not that easy to function in front of a live crowd. So while there were many valiant efforts, the only thing happening was crowds of people watching men publicly humiliate themselves with bored girls trying to soothe the egos of their guys.

I was way too familiar with that sort of soothing. So we went into the chess room. I recognized all the players. They were famous chess players, all former US champions, grandmasters, etc. My mind was going to explode. Live sex in one room, grandmasters in another. I was standing on the periphery of my ideal surreal fantasy world where I couldn't quite enter and enjoy myself for some reason. You want to touch the single breast in a strip club, the gold buried underneath Ft. Knox, the fringe of light from an eclipse but all just too far for me to reach.

I went into another room (the whole party was a maze of rooms) and I was surprised to see a good friend of mine there. He was about 55 years old and used to run the most popular cable music TV station. We were working together on a deal so I had just seen him earlier that day. This was turning into a midnight of coincidence and I was Cinderella at the ball.

He was kissing the neck of a girl that he'd been dating for a few weeks. She was about twenty five years old and very beautiful. Long curly brown hair, big eyes, big breasts. He had just been telling me the other day that she told him she loved him more than she ever loved anyone before. He was very proud to tell me this. He was thirty years older than her. He wanted me to react but I had no idea what to say. That's great, I told him.

She wanted him to hook her up with a translation job in Saudi Arabia since we were in the process of pitching some Middle Eastern investors on a project we were working on. Apparently there were some languages she could translate but I never learned what they were.

He didn't see me when I walked into the room. He was too busy kissing her neck and breasts. He was fervent, anxious, groping. She was looking straight up at the ceiling while his mouth was all over her. I watched her big eyes blink. I thought to myself, she really is beautiful.

She was looking the way you look when blood is being taken from you and you look the other way. Then she saw me staring at them and she quickly started kissing my friend back. Quick pecks all over his face. She had thick red lipstick. Her kisses left red bruises all over his face. I left the room before he could see me. I was embarrassed at the whole thing. Embarrassed that I had been caught staring. Embarrassed for him. For her. Embarrassed for everyone.

I wanted something fun to happen to me at the party. I saw a girl I had long had a crush on but she was surrounded by about ten guys. How many coincidences could happen at one party with me unable to do anything about it? I was like in a dream. I couldn't talk to anyone even though everything around me was a combination of fake and fun. The live sex, the chess in the next room, my 55 year old friend kissing his lipstick girl, chess girl I had a crush on. Ylon had disappeared into the mess of people and I couldn't find him again. I didn't see him for over a year after that. Next time I saw him he was divorced. I barely even knew he was married.

I felt like I was surrounded by people LIVING LIFE but I

was dead inside. I left the party around two in the morning and started to walk home. I was scared that thirty years later I could be living a fake life kiss groping some fake girl, oblivious to her just staring bored at the ceiling. Doesn't matter if you ran MTV for ten minutes. She's still going to stare at the ceiling until she's caught.

Sometimes age only makes your bad habits worse. The false wisdom we supposedly get is just bad habit after bad habit, impacted together, a thick sedimentary rock. A diamond-tipped drill can't break it.

I wanted to just get back to my apartment that I was destined to lose but that loss was still in the future. My apartment was as fake as the rest but I didn't know it until the science fiction future. I would find some comfort there. A book to read before going back to sleep. Quiet.

At one point, two in the morning, walking up Leonard Street on the way home from the party, I thought I heard someone walking quickly behind me. As if trying to catch up to me. I turned around expecting to see someone but nobody was there.

I was all alone.

THE DAY STOCKPICKR WAS GOING TO GO OUT OF BUSINESS – A STORY OF FRIENDSHIP

My site, Stockpickr.com, had 24 hours before it was going to go out of business and then I would probably have to kill myself. I had passed the 2 year point on a life insurance policy where it was now ok to kill myself so that my kids would still get the $4 million in the policy. It was Martin Luther King Day, 2007. He had a dream.

My site was anti-news. And I write for all the news sites. Get rid of me if you want. But you know you scare and panic people until they wake up with stomach pains at 4 in the morning. Just so you could sell another $1.25 with the next nightmare headline. And then you dump them and move onto the next panic.

So I made a finance site with everything but news. The only one. And thestreet.com had just announced it, and Jim Cramer was mentioning it every day on TV. And I knew that once Martin Luther King Day passed, I was going to go out of business.

Because you get what you pay for and I had reached across the planet to hire Indian programmers to program my site. And every time Jim Cramer mentioned the website on TV we crashed. We couldn't handle the load. It wasn't rocket science. I'm a computer programmer. I should've just done it myself. But I hired a bunch of Jainists in Bangalore instead. One day they had a religious holiday. The other day the power went out so nobody was at work.. And finally I get ahold of them at 3 in the morning on Saturday night.

"Please. Please," I said to Arvind, "you have to fix this problem by Monday because Tuesday Cramer's going to mention the site again and if we go down we're out of business. You can't have a site go down anymore else people don't trust it."

"We will fix it," they said, "don't worry." And I waited. All Sunday morning I kept hitting reload. It was slow. I knew it wasn't fixed. "Don't worry, James. You worry too much," Arvind said, "we will fix it." I called up ten friends and we'd click simultaneously and the site will go down. "We're testing stuff," the Indians said, "it might go down but we know what the problem is. We're fixing it."

Monday morning I woke up. I had a letter from Arvind in India. In Bangalore. I've since been to Bangalore. At three in the morning their time, driving from Bangalore to Mysore. When are we going to get on the highway I kept wondering. Everywhere you went seemed like a side street. And random men and women walking along the side all night long. Men peeing on the side of the road. And little carts where the men would hang around drinking whatever. The cab driver had to stop and disappear for awhile and I stood outside thinking, "here I am". I could just disappear and nobody would know, nobody would find me.

But that was years later.

Monday morning. 2007. Martin Luther King day. Letter from Arvind: "I'm sorry, James. But we have to give up. It's late here and we could not figure out the problem. I'm really sorry but we have no idea what the problem is."

And I had 24 hours approximately before I was sure I was out of business. When you are running a business, every detail counts. Your customers are not forgiving. Your competitors laugh in your face. Your benefactors deny they ever knew you. Your programmers move on to their next project and remove your name from their client list.

Your friends say, "well maybe your next business". Your children want to play, not knowing that their lives, too, hang in the balance. But they don't really care because ultimately they move on and leave their parents behind, move on to exciting new lives as artists, lovers, professional whatever, saying, "I had a father once."

So at 7am I made the call. I called Chet. Super Chet. I hadn't spoken to him in at least eight years. His phone number was listed in Boston so I called him. He was the single best pro-grammer on the planet. And he was born in India although raised in Texas.

I'll give you one example. When IBM was hosting the live streaming Olympics in 1996 on the web their servers kept going down. Who did they call? Not their 10,000 person IT depart-ment. They called Chet in his apartment in the Upper West Side. He took his little computer and wrote some sort of networking protocol between his computer and 20 other IBM mainframes around the world. The Olympics was saved. IBM was saved.

Chet lived wherever he wanted. He worked on whatever he wanted. IBM didn't want him to ever leave so they agreed to everything he ever asked for. He put out fires for them. That's what he still does to this day.

We had worked together in 1988. But that's another story. In 1996 he would hang out at my first company and do all the spare programming we needed on the weekends. For free. He just liked doing it. That was his weekend fun.

One time in 1996 he called me while I was out on the town and he was programming. "James! Why did you write the code this way? It's like spaghetti. You took up 10 pages of code when just a few lines would've done it."

"Chet," I asked him. "Is the client standing right there next to you?"

"Yes," he said.

"THEN SHUT THE FUCK UP!"

"Ahh," he said, "got it!" And he hung up the phone.

Martin Luther King day: 2007, 6am. I call Chet for the first time since 1999. "Chet, it's James." "James?" "Look, no time to update. I hope all is well but I need your help badly."

I explained the whole problem to him in about three minutes. I think I was crying.

"Ok, ok, ok," he said, and he asked a couple of technical questions about how the site was built. I answered the best I could.

"Ok," he said, "here's the problem: I have a plane to catch to Paris at around 4pm so I really only have until 2pm. I'm giving a talk there and I can't skip it. But give me the phone number of the Indians and give me access to all the servers." I gave him all of the passwords.

"I can't do this from home. I'm going to do this from the office. I'll call you in twenty minutes."

"PLEASE FUCKING FIX THIS!" I said, "THEY'RE FROM INDIA. JUST LIKE YOU! YOU CAN DEAL WITH THEM!" I'm not pretty in a panic.

"Ok, ok, James. You have. To calm. Down." he said, "give me twenty minutes to get dressed and get into the office." It was 6am and he had a plane to Paris to catch.

By noon that day he had spoken to the Indians, he had rewritten half the code, he gave them detailed instructions about what they had been doing wrong, he advised me on how to keep calm in moments like this and what I should be looking to do long-term to fix the site. He did all of this even though the site was written in a programming language he had never used before. On the way to the office he somehow learned the programming language.

By noon that day the problem was fixed. The site never crashed again.

By 4pm he was on a flight to Paris. When he got there I called him. "Chet, I can't thank you enough. I want to give you a piece of the company. You deserve it."

"No way, James," he said, "remember in 1995 when we were on the 42nd Street subway platform underneath Times Square?"

"No," I said.

"I was going on and on about distributed objects, blah blah and you said, 'Chet! Shut up with that. Its boring. You should be doing the Internet and nothing else. That's what is going to make your career.' "

"I don't remember," I said.

"Well that conversation changed my life. I switched everything to the Internet. You were right! And its changed my life ever since."

I didn't know what to say. Maybe I vaguely remembered. He continued:

"Consider the favor returned."

MY BLIND DATE GONE BAD

I had an idea and I knew some people were going to be hurt by it. But first I called my friend, Amy, to see if she liked the idea and wanted to participate. She was in. Then I called Michel, for video, and Adrian, for audio, and we needed Francois. For security. Just in case things got a little crazy.

The idea was this. Amy would put an ad in the Village Voice. "girl seeking date", etc. Then guys would respond to the ad and she'd pick the most interesting ones and she'd also pick the restaurant they would meet at. Michel would wire up video all over the restaurant and Adrian would do the audio. We'd then videotape the date without the date knowing.

First, some notes. Amy is: "Girl whose name was a curse". I had a crush on her. She was also extraordinarily funny. A standup comedian at heart. She knew the date was going to be recorded and she knew how to get people talking.

Michel was my brother in law. We started our first business, Reset, together. We must've made a million websites together back when making websites was a bit harder than it is now. Or maybe it was easier then. Less technology. Either way, we started with Americanexpress.com and HBO.com and worked our way up from there.

Adrian was the son of the former Minister of Health under Ceausescu in Romania. He was literally from Transylvania and, if you met him, you would know that instantly. He defected from Romania when he was a famous photographer there photographing underage girls doing things. Ceausescu swore to Adrian's mother that he would find Adrian and bring him back. But he was never found again.

Francois was formerly in the French Foreign Legion and was now about 90 years old but didn't look a day over fifty. No matter how many vasectomies he had he kept having more children. It was a problem. But he was a big guy.

We had two dates with all of us spread over two tables. Amy and her date at one table. Francois, Michel, Adrian, and I at the next table. Doing what we usually did. Listening in on the people around us. The only one who had no clue was Amy's date.

On date number one the guy confessed he was torn between feelings of being gay and being straight. He was unsure if he could be both at the same time. Amy touched his hand once and he lit up like a struck match. At the end she asked him to sign a release form and, surprised, he did. The next day he called her up and left a voicemail where he was yelling, "life is to be lived. Not televised!"

The next date the guy received a telephone call in the middle of the date. It was from his wife.

Afterwards, Amy asked him to sign a release form but he said he would only sign it if she would sleep with him. So we didn't get his release form signed.

Michel edited all the videos together. I pitched the idea to HBO Independent Productions. "We love it!" a guy named Dave said to me. I don't remember his last name. He never called me back. I called him every day, thinking "this is the day that Dave changes my life." I was sitting in a cubicle at HBO in the IT Department. My life is going to change today. "One second," Dave's secretary would say to me. I was calling HBO even though I worked at HBO. But Dave was in LA. "I love it," Dave said to me the first time we spoke. I held onto that. Love is an important emotion. "Dave said he is going to call you right back," the secretary would say to me. And I would feel relieved. Because he was going to call me RIGHT BACK. Only he never did.

Finally I called Dave and said, "This is Randy, I need to talk to Dave." Randy was "Randy" in "How I hacked MTV.com". They both went to Harvard together.

Dave got on the phone, "Raaandddyyy!" he said. "Actually, Dave, its James".

So Dave had to explain to me what happened. "Politics," he said. "You're already pitching one show to another part of HBO. So they want first look on this show." Not only was I sitting in a little cubicle in HBO's IT department, I was running an entire company on the side and pitching two TV shows to two different parts of HBO. I was on the phone all day long trying to juggle things. The guy in the cubicle next to me once came over to me, "Whatever you are doing, I don't want to know about it."

So I went to Sheila Nevins, who, as I mentioned before, was in charge of all of HBO's shows on prostitution PLUS she was head of HBO Family Programming (for the kids). I was already pitching a show to her but she was upset I went to HBO Independent Productions. "I love the idea of this show," she said to me over lunch in HBO's Executive Dining Room, "but we can't do this. It's too mean."

So that was my idea. And some people got hurt.

Hitchhiker's Guide to the Universe

Its dangerous to hitchhike and I'll never do it again after my initial experiences. I was employee #8 at a company called FORE Systems. I was the worst employee there. They thought I could write the instruction manuals for their fiber-optic products. I was miserable at this.

The founder of the company, Robert Sansom, once called me into his office and said to me, "you need to take a little more pride in your work". Eventually I built a version of the video game "Missile Command" that they were able to use as a demo for their cards. The company went public and eventually sold to Marconi for $4.5 billion. I would've made a lot of money but I hated it so I quit after only about five months there.

I used to get a ride to work every morning from my neighbor who worked there. But one time we exchanged information on our salaries. Don't ever do this. When I told him mine he hit his steering wheel and said, "damn!" since it was clear to everyone that I was worth $0 or even negative. He didn't tell me what his salary was. That afternoon he told me he couldn't take me home anymore from work.

There was no way I was going to drive home from work. I don't drive. And I didn't mind the bus in the morning but I didn't want to take it in the evening. Weirdoes are on the bus at night.

All day long every day I'd be excited for the end of the day. Who would I meet today? What adventure would I embark on? Would I end up dead in an alley in some random town on the outskirts of Pittsburgh? Would I be cast in a movie? Or would I end up knighted by Queen Elizabeth? Anything can happen!

I stood at the same spot on the highway each day at 4:50. So the same people would see me. One guy picked me up three times over a three-month period. He was overweight and was telling me how he wanted to get in shape the first time. He asked what I did. I told him I was a writer but that I had three unpublished novels so it wasn't working out too well for me.

The second time he told me he was in big trouble. It was about a month later. He slept with his wife's sister and she had found out. The sister had just told his wife that morning. You can ask, why did the sister tell his wife? But sisters have a way of doing that. I think he wanted advice from me but I didn't really know what to say. "I thought it was going to improve my marriage," he said to me. "I had lost the attraction to my wife so I thought this would be a way to reclaim it."

The third time he picked me up it was about a month later. His wife was in the car with him. "Hey," he turned to his wife after I had gotten in the back, "this is the guy I was telling you about!" They were on their way to a born-again Christian meeting. "It's totally revitalized our marriage. You should go to these meetings with us." When I got out of the car he gave me some pamphlets. "You have to come with us to the next meeting." His wife didn't say anything the entire ride.

Another time a girl picked me up. "You aren't going to rape

me or anything," she said when she rolled down the window.
Then she laughed. "I don't know why I just said that." She got
out of the car and walked around and opened up my car door,
which had been unlocked. "I don't know why I just did that,"
she said.

We talked all the back into Pittsburgh. She had dark red hair.
Freckles. By the time she dropped me off I was in love with
her. Because that's the way I operated. She worked in a doctor's office and fortunately there was only one "Mary" there so I
called the next day and asked her out.

At dinner later that week she said to me, "I have some friends
you need to meet. You'd like them. They are very interesting."
And it occurred to me she viewed me in a completely different
way than I viewed myself. I wasn't a mediocre employee of
a fiber-optic company on the outskirts of Pittsburgh. I was an interesting person . I was "the hitchhiker". I was "that guy I was
telling you about".

The next day I called her at her home. I wanted to go out
again. And marry her. She wasn't home. So 15 minutes later I
called again. Next time I waited 25 minutes. But then after that
I called after 10 minutes. Where could she be? I called again.
After about three hours of this she picked up the phone, "Was
that you calling all of these times?" "Uhh, I think I called a few
times. But maybe not every time. If that's what you are referring
to." I never saw her again.

Another time, in the morning, I hitchhiked with the guy who
"invented" the smiley emoticon, Scott Fahlman. Although at the
time I did now know that was what he was famous for. I knew
who he was because he was a professor at the same graduate
school I had been thrown out of two years earlier. Only later did
I realize his contribution to society.

I got so good at hitchhiking I would race friends to restaurants. They would take their cars and I would have to hitchhike. I got very good at projecting an instant sense of safety and vulnerability. People would know I had no plans to kill them. But even though you aren't going to kill the person who picks you up you also have to give off the vibe that you would be interesting to talk to for five minutes. These skills came in quite handy in business.

That was the deal I had to provide every time someone stopped. No killing or raping. And fast, scintillating conversation. But other than getting from point A to point B, I wasn't allowed to expect anything back. Other than a tiny story about feeling humiliated by a girl with dark red hair.

HOW TO WIN AT MONOPOLY EVERY TIME

When I was in 7th grade, I got a letter asking me if I wanted to go to an experimental summer program for 13 year olds at Duke University after I took the SATs.

Everyone there was smarter than me. The first day there, one person told me he was building a computer in his dorm room. Another kid was one of the youngest chess masters in the country.

The idea of the program was that people only really learn when they are immersed in something.

My subject was "Math". So in a three-week period I passed through all of high school math and one year of Calculus.

From 8am until about 5pm you sat in a room and went at your own pace. Teaching assistants stood around and would help you if you needed it. Then you would take tests to advance to the next level whenever you wanted.

I ended up last in the class.

The second summer I went back I took Statistics. We figured out all the statistics for Monopoly.

I have three words for you: St. James. Place. Then build as many hotels as you can on the Orange group and CHEAPER. Forget about the expensive stuff.

That third summer I ruined my life.

I liked a girl. Marcy.

Statistics were obliterated when she spoke to me. The odds never went in my favor. She wouldn't let me own St. James Place.

For the rest of high school I was obsessed with a girl liking me. Any girl.

So I tried to get good at things. I tried to get good at tricks. At gimmicks.

Maybe if I were special, if I had a gift I could give, then a girl would bless me her special gift back. People would like me.

Chess is probably the wrong thing to get good at if you want a girl to like you.

Breakdancing was slightly better. But if you're Jewish, with glasses, and braces, then it sort of looks funny when you try to breakdance.

And what completely failed was trying to learn hypnosis so you could command girls to undress in front of you. That NEVER worked.

These were all gimmicks.

The only way to get good at something is to completely immerse yourself in it - to the outside world, immersion is the same as magic.

You can only immerse yourself in something you love.

Else you won't be able to get good. The 10,000 hour rule will fail.

With immersion + love you can get great in much less than 10,000 hours.

Lesson: Only do the things you love. Otherwise, you're

running on a treadmill. And the treadmill will stop when you least expect it, cracking happiness into pieces.

I still try to do too many gimmicks to get people to love me. But I think I'm getting better at avoiding doing the things I don't love with people I don't love. It's a daily practice.

Right now, all I want to do is immerse myself in these Facebook status updates. That sounds stupid but it's true.

I love stringing words together. How to connect them so they tick-tock like a clock. I love to read writers who really know how to WRITE. That's what obliterates me now.

Or maybe I'll learn to just enjoy a good book. Take a walk by the river with Claudia. Watch the sun set. And learn to love looking at the mountains without always having to climb them.

MY VISIT TO THE WHITE HOUSE

I put in a call to The White House. 202-456-1414. I asked for the President's office. The operator patched me through to a secretary. I asked her if I could interview the President. My dad was taking me to Washington DC for my 12th birthday and I wanted to stop by.

The secretary was very kind. She said the President was busy with [I forget if it was the coal miner's strike or the Iranian hostage crisis] and wouldn't be able to meet. So I asked for a signed photo of Amy Carter. Which was sent to me.

I then called back The White House. I asked for Rex Scouten. He was Chief Usher of the White House and had worked in The White House since the Truman years. I saw his name in "The World Almanac and Book of Facts". He got on the phone. I asked him if I could interview him.

He said, "sure!" and when my dad and I visited, we went through a special door to meet him and he gave us a tour of The White House, even the areas where the First Family lived.

My dad saw the President walking down a hallway but I didn't see him. My dad tried to get me to look but I wasn't paying attention and missed the President.

Anyway, when I got back home I lied and told all my friends I saw the President.

Then we went to Capitol Hill. I had called ahead and we met with many Senators and Congressmen.

We met Paul Tsongas, for instance, who was a Senator from Massachusetts and later ran for President. Tsongas was famous for being the poorest person in the Senate.

He also was famous for saying, "no one ever said on their deathbed I wish I had spent more time at work". He quit the Senate when he was diagnosed with cancer.

While my dad was busy with a business appointment, I went to visit Birch Bayh, the Senator from Indiana. It was his birthday too. His staff brought out his birthday cake and they sang Happy Birthday to both of us.

I can't imagine letting my kids wander around Washington DC by themselves at the age of 12.

We had so much more freedom then. We could ride subways, explore cities, ride our bikes on highways, take rides with strangers, shoplift, explore the woods, smoke cigarettes, whatever we wanted. We were energy uncorked.

Kids aren't allowed to have adventures anymore.

But adults stop having them also. We start worrying about the bills. We start regretting the past. I was at a party last night. Did I say the wrong thing? Did they like me?

When you skim a book you notice a word or two per page. Maybe sometimes you read a paragraph.

But you finish the book super fast. You're done! Finished! And you think it's an accomplishment.

Sometimes I find myself skimming life. Not noticing all the words right in front of me.

Saying "yes" to too many things I don't want to do. Thinking too much of past or future. Trying very hard to just finish. That's why time seems to move faster as we get older.

I'm going to try and stop time today. Or at least slow it down. I don't know.

Today will be an ordinary day. But maybe I can try to make every moment in it be extraordinary.

GO WITH THE FLOW: I'M A LUCKY GUY

The last time I went to the dentist's office, I was on the Jay Leno show.

A month before, the dentist had said, "Your mouth is the worst train wreck I have ever seen. We need to take out two teeth, fix up some cavities, do a root canal, and wipe out your gum disease. We're going to have to spread it out over multiple appointments."

"Does this mean I have bad breath?" I asked.

"Probably," he said.

"Will I be able to get a prescription for Percocet?" I asked.

"Probably," he said.

Suddenly I was calling the shots. "Ok, we're not going to spread this out through several appointments. We're going to do it in one go. I need an anesthesiologist, your best oral surgeon. I need my wife here. And I need two prescriptions of Percocet to keep away the pain once it's over."

"Two prescriptions?" he asked.

"Is this a dentist's office? Are you a dentist? Am I getting teeth pulled? Do you prescribe Percocet?"

He scheduled everything. He was very happy. I have no dental insurance. A $6000 appointment to clean up my breath and get Percocet.

Plus, good dental hygiene is related to longer life. Did you know the leading cause of suicide in the 1800s was dental pain? My dentist did not know that. I knew that.

I am full of facts about suicide.

I love that moment when they stick that thing in your arm and they say "ok, count down from ten..." And you don't remember even saying "six" and you start to wake up.

I swear to god I was going to fight it. I was going to make it to zero.

But by the time I was at 'five' i was already waking up. The oral surgery was over. There was crap all over my mouth. Claudia was standing right next to me. She was laughing.

"You were just talking about golf to the nurse. Do you even play golf?" she said.

"I don't think so. Maybe I played in an alternate reality I had to visit. The reality where I am mega-champion of everything."

"Oh," she said, "they also pulled out another tooth."

"WHAT!"?

"Yeah," she said, "I don't understand what they said. You had a fifth wisdom tooth or something."

"I must be very wise," I said, "you should maybe pay a little more attention when I say things."

What else can I say. The Percocet (only one prescription) kicked in nicely until...

The hiccups kicked in. Maybe I had oxygen pumped into me or something. I started hiccupping around 6pm that night and didn't stop until I fell asleep around 9pm. It was really annoying me. Every five seconds. Hiccup.

My kids were laughing. We tried everything to stop me from

hiccupping. They pretended to be vampires scaring me. I got a paper bag and breathed into it until i thought I was going to pass out. I did a headstand. I tried to vomit. But I kept hiccupping.

"This is ruining my Percocet high," I said and started to cry.

Then at two in the morning I woke up and I wasn't hiccuping but my mouth was really hurting. I mean it really started to HURT.

So, of course, I grabbed my cell phone and checked emails.

"Congrats!" was the first message.

"Don't worry. All publicity is good publicity," said another message.

"Great stuff on Jay Leno! He said your name right!" was the third message.

The fourth message was from Scott Mednick who once ran for Governor of California and was also my boss in a previous lifetime. He also produced one of the Superman movies. He said, "I was there when they were cutting the footage. I couldn't believe it when I saw you."

What the...?

Apparently Jay Leno had made a little joke that night.

A video clip, a song: "Too Old To Look Like Harry Potter." Cut with a clip from me I had made a few months earlier for CNBC. The whole thing is on YouTube. The audience was laughing quite a bit.

My mouth was on fire. It was like someone blew up an explosive on my teeth.

"What's going on," Claudia mumbled in her sleep.

"I'm too old to look like Harry Potter," I said. And my mouth hurt. But at least my breath was good and so I leaned over and kissed her.

It was a new day. I had no idea what new adventure would happen but I was ready for it.

Everything Is Funny All The Time

One time my neighbor said, "you have to come in and meet my boss. He can put up to a hundred million dollars into your fund."

So we went into town and met his boss. We spoke for quite a bit. I felt like I was impressing the boss. Maybe this would be a new mentor for me. I felt happy.

He was the largest hedge fund manager in the world.

Then the boss said, "James, I like you. If you ever want to work here, we'd hire you. But we can't put money into your fund."

"Ok," I said because I never disagreed with anyone about anything.

But I felt disappointed. Why can't I do anything right? Why didn't he like me?

"For us everything is reputation," my friend's boss continued.

"I have no idea where you are actually putting that money," he said. "And the last thing this business needs," said the owner of the business, "is for Bernard Madoff Securities to appear on the front page of the *Wall Street Journal.*"

After I left, other people called me. "Did you meet him?" one random friend asked.

"Yeah," I said, "very nice guy."

"He's the best fund manager ever."

I said I didn't know. I felt crushed.

Much later, that very same friend, who now manages over a billion, said to me, "we always knew he was a fraud."

—ɯ—

Another time I started a business called "Junglesmash". The idea was that I pick a product, like "Crest toothpaste" and people would submit 2 minute ads they would make for Crest Toothpaste and I would give $2000 to whatever ad I judged to be the best ad.

A lot of people submitted ads. What's funny is that Procter & Gamble actually submitted about ten ads for Crest. I felt like this could be a real business. It could take off and would disrupt the entire ad business. Crowdsourcing ads!

Once it took off I would set up an exchange where companies could put up products and sponsor contests and I would take a cut.

I would be like Don Draper 2.0.

But it rained a lot that quarter. And I was getting a divorce. Divorce is always good but right in the middle of it there are parts that are unbelievably painful.

So I'd sit in a hammock and try to read a book and fall asleep and then it would rain and I would wake up soaked.

I'd forget about Junglesmash and eventually the site, the company, the idea of disrupting the ad business washed away with the rain and my depression. You can still see some of the ads submitted at junglesmash dot blogspot dot com.

One ad was very funny. Set to Star Wars music, two kids fought with their toothbrush light sabers. Crest versus Colgate. Crest won. I sent them two thousand dollars for winning that month.

I still think this is a good idea. Someone should do it. For me, when I think about it I just think of all that rain. I think of sitting in the bookstore by the local museum, eating a scone and trying to will myself to death. It didn't work.

The business idea wasn't a hoax. Me thinking I could function like a normal human being then was beyond funny.

—m—

Being born was the only serious thing I ever did. After that, we're on our own, trying to survive. Trying to get the joke.

I try new things all the time. I want to get the joke. I want to find the humor in everything.

My daughter one time told me she wanted to be a clown when she grew up because "then I would make people laugh while I made money".

I hope she does this.

Some people list the things they are grateful for. This is a good list to do.

But I try to also list the things around me that are funny. The things that are more than funny. The things that are ludicrous.

This is a more fun list. This is the list that lights my brain on fire. It takes practice but it's worth it.

Because if you can't find the humor in everything around you, then eventually you find out too late that the joke is on you.

HOW STEVIE COHEN
CHANGED MY LIFE

I wanted to change everything and have it all be better. I was sitting in the waiting area of Stevie Cohen's office (the biggest hedge fund billionaire out there) and I knew that within a few minutes my life would change.

Every now and then you have those moments when its up to one person to turn your life upside down and make it better. Sometimes they don't even realize how much power they have in their hands. Sheila Nevins, the executive producer of all of HBO's TV shows about prostitutes (and the head of their Family Programming division) once had that power over me. She would look at a 45-minute video and could decide "Yes" or "No" and my whole life could change. That was in 1998. She said, "No".

So now I'm in 2004, and I had been trading about $27 million allocated to me from various hedge funds and investors. It's hard to build a business so I wanted to switch to trading for Stevie Cohen's SAC Capital, the biggest hedge fund in the world. Stevie Cohen was the best investor in the world and people working for him could make 10s of millions of dollars a year.

At first I emailed him. I didn't have his email address so I tried various combinations ofstevecohen@sac.com, steve@sac.com, cohen@sac.com, etc. I sent about 30 emails to 30 different combinations of the above. No response. The next month I did it again. And again. Finally, after a year of doing this, there was a response: "What's your IM". So Stevie Cohen, the best investor in the world, with $3bb of his own money in SAC Capital, and I started to IM with each other.

I explained my approach and he wanted to meet. So a few weeks later a car service took me to Stamford, CT. I'm not allowed to drive. Particularly in Connecticut. But that's another story.

I waited for about a half hour. It was near the close of the trading day so I assumed he was busy. People were walking in and out of the building. They were all wearing these fleece jackets that said SAC Capital on them. They were like a big family. They all loved each other. I could tell. I wanted to be part of the family also. So I could love them and they could love me. We would joke around at lunchtime. Maybe we would make fun of Cohen and all laugh but all nervously looking around to make sure he wasn't there. Slowly we would get to know each other and, when they were comfortable with me, maybe they would invite me over to dinner to meet their family. "This is that new guy I was telling you about. Thank God Stevie Cohen hired him!"

Finally, someone came to get me, "He's ready for you now." She brought me to another person who wasn't Stevie Cohen. And then this person took me to Stevie Cohen's office. His office was the size of a small football stadium. I had always heard he sat out in the center of the trading floor with his traders but this was his private office. If he were Dr. Strange from Marvel Comics this would be known as his Sanctum Sanctorum.

He was sitting on the couch.

"So this is the famous street.com columnist!" he said. I sat down across from him.

"Why do you want to start trading for me?" he asked.

"Its hard to trade, raise money, manage a business," I said. "I think the economics work a lot better if I'm managing money for you."

"You're absolutely right," he said.

We went over my strategy. I gave him a copy of my book, "Trade Like a Hedge Fund" that just came out. My basic strategy that I traded was similar: look for patterns in the market that have worked over the past 5, 10, even 50 years. If those patterns occur again, then trade them.

"I like this approach," he said, and he took my book from me, "I like to look at market history."

He got up. The meeting was over after about ten minutes of talking. One thing he told me as he got up was that this was his worst trading day in about six months. But he didn't seem bothered. Or at least I couldn't tell. Which is very different from how I react when I have my worst trading day in six months. When I have my worst trading day in six months, everyone around me can tell. They can smell it on me. That's what separates the greatest trader ever from a trader like me.

We started to walk together out the door, down the hallway. "Lets do this," he said, " why don't you instant message me before you do a trade for the next few weeks. We'll see how it goes in real time."

We both walked out together. I was embarrassed just in case he would see the dirty white cadillac that the car service had delivered me in. He stepped into his shiny new car and waved goodbye. I was sort of hoping he would invite me over for dinner. Maybe he could show me his art collection.

I forget what kind of car it was. Lets just say it was a BMW. I was surprised nobody talked to him at all as we were leaving even though we passed quite a few people in the hallway. At SAC Capital, everyone communicates psychically. There's no need for actual "hellos" and "goodbyes". I assume there's a lot of hugging there also, but that they didn't do it in front of strangers like me. But I kind of wanted Stevie Cohen to hug me before he got into his car. "It's going to be ok," he would say to me. But that didn't happen.

The next day, right around 9:29 am before I was going to make my first trade of the day I instant messaged him the trade. He wrote back, "Thanks". I'm not exaggerating: about 50 trades in a row had worked out for me at that point. It was June 2004, and I hadn't had a down month since July, 2003. Not even a down week. Until that trade.

And the next seven trades after it.

I was totally disheartened. It was like being impotent and telling the girl, "this has never happened to me before." Stevie Cohen was THAT GIRL.

"Don't worry", Cohen IM-ed me. "Just relax. We can try again in an hour." Actually, he didn't IM that. He IM-ed. "Don't worry. This happens."

But at some point I just stopped sending him trades. And a few days later he IMed, "where are you???" but I didn't respond to that. I was ashamed.

MY TAKEAWAYS:

A) Go for it. If you want to work for someone. Email them today.

B) Be persistent. Make you have something to say: but say it every month. Until they respond. At some point if you deliver enough value, they will respond.

C) **Research.** I knew everything about Cohen before my meeting with him. I had planned, prepared, researched everything I could so that I could leave that meeting with my goal intact: a follow-up

D) **The One Person Rule.** Never have your happiness dependent on a yes or no decision from one person. At the very least: diversify the people who are important enough to do that.

E) **Bad day.** When you have a bad day, the professionals just roll with it and keep the same emotional demeanor as the good days.

F) **Stay in the game:** This I didn't do. I should've kept IMing trades. I should've somehow stayed in the game. I let shame get the better of me.

Recently I wrote to Cohen again. He was having problems in the media. His ex-wife was all over the place. We all know the drill. I told him his media wasn't being handled correctly. I told him he should write a book about his life. It would be a fascinating read and set the story straight. I told him I would help him write it. I pictured us high-fiving and laughing over a glass of wine in front of some of the famous Picassos he owns. His wife is of Hispanic origin. So is mine! High five! Jews rock!

He responded and we wrote back and forth for a while. I won't respond with what he said due to his privacy issues. But finally he said, "I don't think anyone would be interested in reading a book about me."

Then I made a big mistake. I wrote back, "it would be the second best-selling business biography ever: after Warren Buffett's biography." Never, NEVER, imply that one billionaire might be a bigger sell than another billionaire.

He never wrote back.

DID I MENTION I WAS ONCE A RESPIRATORY THERAPIST?

Did I mention the time I was a professional respiratory thera-pist? My girlfriend's sister's boyfriend's father heard that I liked to write. He had an idea for a novel based on his life experience as a doctor but for several reasons he couldn't write it himself. So he called me, introduced himself, explained the situation and asked if I would like to write it. It would involve pretending to be a respiratory therapist and working in a hospital for a week so I could see what was really going on behind the scenes. He would also pay me for my time. Of course I said yes.

Why couldn't this man write it himself? Several reasons:

A) He was a prominent doctor in perhaps the most famous hospital in the country. He didn't want to risk exposing his position but he still wanted the word out.

B) He didn't think he had any ability as a writer. This is never the case. Everyone can tell their story. But if someone says, "I can't do this but I'm willing to pay you to do it" then who am I to disagree?

C) He was busy. He had patients all day long and he was happy with the knowledge that he was a great doctor. Writing a book would interfere with his time he spent helping patients.

D) And, perhaps more importantly he was dying and nobody knew that. Not even his son who had indirectly introduced us. I was to tell no one, he said, because he had not even told his wife and family yet. He was hoping the book would make some money and that this money would help take care of his family after he was gone. I didn't understand the disease he was dying from. It's the opposite of leukemia, he said. Instead of affecting the white cells like leukemia does, my illness kills the red cells. I have somewhere between six and twelve months to live, he told me.

So I arranged to take a week off of work, and stay in a small hotel near where the doctor lived and worked. He was upset at the cavalier way in which doctors and nurses treated their patients in his hospital. He felt the medical industry had transformed from an industry where people helped people to an industry where professionals milked their patients dry of all of their money while providing inadequate care. Again, the hospital he was at wasn't a small facility but one of the most major and important facilities in the country. The type of hospital people say they are going to when they want to convince everyone else that they are receiving the best possible care for their ills and nothing was being left to chance. And I was going to be a respiratory therapist there for a week.

The first day he picked me up at the hotel and we ate at an IHOP while he explained the basics. I was going to pretend I was finishing up training as a respiratory therapist and wanted to see what it was like to work in a hospital. Another respiratory therapist, a woman named Jenny, was in on what I was doing and would show me the ropes for the week. She was good friends with the doctor and agreed with him that the medical industry she had signed up for was not what she thought it was.

And there it was. I spent the week going from room to room, often to check in with Jenny on people who were critically ill (hence their need for someone to come in and check that they were breathing ok). I was hardly ever on my own although occasionally I would help old people walk up and down their hallways until they were out of breath. In the lounge where the doctors and nurses relaxed I would hear all the clichéd stories. Doctors describing their new cars while flirting with nurses, the other respiratory therapists sharing the occasional horror story about how the one time that tracheotomy was botched, the tube removed and the hole never covered up, suffocating the patient. But I didn't see anything grossly negligent (other than allowing me to wander in and out of patients rooms, checking their equipment to make sure everything was A-ok).

What I did notice above all else was my breath. I never really thought about the concept of "breathing" before. It just sort of happens. But when I was walking these old people up and down the hallways, listening carefully as their breath became more and more shallow to the point where it was non-existent, or when I was checking on people's equipment, where the sounds of artificial breath filled up an entire room until it seemed every piece of equipment was breathing and keeping the patient alive, I became painfully aware of how I was breathing.

I was a horrible breather!

I realized how shallow my own breaths were most of the time. Sometimes I even felt like I was gasping for air along with the patients.

Breathing just sort of happens. We can't do anything about it. Our bodies do it with or without us. Take a moment to breathe deeply three times and really notice the breath. Who is doing it? You? Your body? Notice it. Notice the end of the breath when you exhale, that brief little moment of empty space before your entire body does a U-turn and forces oxygen back into it. We can't stop breathing but what's going on in our head effects how we breathe. What's slowing the breath down? If you're scared, your breath changes. If you are sad or happy, your breath changes. What's changing the rate of your breath right now? You? Notice it some more and breathe deeply. Three breaths.

All of the self-help books in the world will never help you if you can't breathe. And if you just take the time to notice your breath occasionally, I really think you'll never need any of the self-help books out there. Just do it again. Three deep breaths. Watch them. My New Year's resolution this year is to pay attention to my breathing. It can't be that hard. Can it?

So my week ended and I felt qualified to speak intelligently about respiratory therapy and the entire medical industry. I had an idea for a plot, wherein someone fools everyone into believing he's a doctor when he's not, but in doing so underlines the ridiculousness of the entire industry. But my friend, the doctor, had an alternative idea where the character based on his was having this torrid affair with the "Jenny" character. I didn't like it and I had a hard time writing someone else's ideas.

But unfortunately it didn't matter. I suddenly became unable to type. I got what I thought was a severe case of Carpal-Tunnel Syndrome where the nerves going into the hand get inflamed whenever you try to type. It's a repetitive stress disorder. I went to a chiropractor, took pain medication, did acupuncture but nothing helped. The doctor kept calling me to see if I had begun writing but I couldn't type at all. The pain was too excruciating. Eventually he stopped calling me. There was nothing I could do. He thought I needed surgery on my hands but I didn't want to do that. Even when he stopped calling me, whenever I looked at the keyboard my hands would start to hurt. The only way I could type out emails or do the computer programming that was my job at the time was to type by holding two pencils and using the erasers to tap on the keys. But I couldn't write a novel that way.

A few months later my girlfriend told me that the doctor had passed away. He had succumbed to that disease that was like the reverse of leukemia. Within a week I was able to type again.

MY NEW YEAR RESOLUTION IN 1995

I was never good with New Year's Resolutions. Every year I wanted things to change so drastically from the prior year that I couldn't even imagine what resolutions would be required in order to make that dangerous and irrevocable leap. New Year's Eve 1994 I was completely lost and frustrated with jobs, relationships, family. One girl had broken up with me long distance after three years of swearing love every day to each other, another job (HBO) was close to firing me because I hadn't done anything there yet, and I owed some $70,000 for my education.

I was playing chess at the Chess Shop on Thompson St New Year's Eve. A girl who I thought was very pretty came in and sat watching my game. She then drew my picture on a napkin. "Five dollars," she said to me, "and I'll sell you this picture." I gave her the $5 simply because a pretty girl had never drawn a picture of me before. She signed it "Elena Van Gogh". "I'm descended from Vincent Van Gogh," she said, and then she left.

The guy I was playing chess with laughed. "That girl is crazy," he said. Nine years later I ran into him on the street on the other side of town. "We played chess on New Year's

142

Eve, 1994."

"How the hell do you remember that?" he said, "I can't even remember what I had for breakfast this morning."

I remember.

Later that night, New Year's Eve, 1994, I was walking towards the Lower East Side. Elias, my roommate (and I mean ROOMmate. The place was about 8 feet by 8 feet) had a "friend" over. I couldn't go home for awhile. I saw Elena was crossing the street. "Hey," I said.

"HEY!" she was excited. "Lets hang out!" So I was game. I had nothing else to do. This was my New Year's resolution. To do things different.

The first thing she wanted to do was get some crack.

I don't smoke, or drink. "Do you have $10?" she said. So we went to a donut shop on 14th and Second Avenue. I waited in the cab while she went in. The cabdriver turned around to take a closer look at me. "Just don't fuck her," he said. She ran out and slammed the car door. "GO ASSHOLE!" she yelled at the cab driver. We were driving towards the "Soho Motel" as far east on Grand Avenue that you can possibly go.

On the FDR drive, "that fucking guy just looked at me," she said and crouched low into the back seat. She pointed to the car next to us. "Those guys are killers."

We got to the Motel and I checked us in. I had a credit card despite my $70,000 in college debt. That's why America is great. We get up to the room. I don't know what I wanted to happen. I wasn't crazy. But then again, maybe I was. "Fuck!" she said, when she opened up the paper bag and pulled out this white nugget and a pipe. "I can't do this without heroin also." She turned on the TV.

"You have to get out for a second!" she screamed at me. "My brother is on the TV screen and he's crazy! Get out! Walk up

and down the hallway. Just GET OUT! COME BACK IN
TEN MINUTES!"

I walked outside the room and up and down the hallway, like
I was told. Sometimes its important to just follow orders. Other
couples were walking around, mumbling to themselves. Everyone was whispering their New Year's resolutions to each other
at the Soho Motel.

Finally, I saw a staircase. Went downstairs and walked out of
the building. I took a cab back to where I lived. Elias was there
by himself. When I told him what had happened he sniffed my
breath. Like maybe he thought I had crack breath or something.
Now he's a fisherman in Rhode Island.

God, thank god I survived being younger. My first New
Year's Resolution for 2011? No drama at all. I don't want to get
married again (I already did that in 2010). I don't want to move
again (did that in 2010). I don't want to make tons of private investments (I have enough, thank you). So many times I walked
the gray tightrope between the light and the darkness. I don't
need light or dark in 2011.

New Year's Day, 1995, sixteen years ago. It was coldest day
in the history of mankind. In Port Authority at 7am old men
were lying on the floor like it was the day after the Apocalypse
and I had been the only one to survive. I took the bus to New
Jersey and my dad picked me up at the stop. He shook my
hand like we were in business together and had just concluded
a very successful deal. I had dinner with my parents. "This is
going to be a great year for you," my mom said to me. And
she was right.

THE ONE REASON WHY FACEBOOK IS WORTH $100 BILLION

Beth Wesloh is getting married. When I was in fifth grade I was in love with her. I knew that because I told her I liked her even more than I liked my grandmother's sister. I had no special feelings at all for my aunt but I figured if I liked a girl as much as a family member then that must mean I was in love with her.

My entire knowledge about love at that time came from "Are you there god, its me Margaret", "Tales of a Fourth Grade Nothing", and, scandalously, "Forever" – all by the Shakespeare of 12 year olds everywhere – Judy Blume.

Beth had red hair, pale skin, an awkward, somewhat offbeat, smile. She moved into town when I was in 4th grade, the day I got glasses. I know this because I refused to lift my head off of the desk, I was so embarrassed about my glasses. How could my parents have done this to me? Cripple me with their lousy vision DNA. Mrs. Osborne, the teacher, kept saying throughout the day, "James, you have to lift your head up off of your desk so Beth, the new girl, can see what you look like." But I had glasses on. So I wasn't moving.

In seventh grade the bigger kids would just randomly punch you right in the face and laugh. Kids got cruel. But in fifth grade it was all about Judy Blume. Kids had crushes for the first time but nobody called it crushes. It was "love". They broke free from the now-awkward communications with their parents who "never understood". They wondered about God and sex and what the older kids did. Lee Applebaum, on my Hebrew school carpool, told my mom, me, and Jennifer F., that his babysitter peed in his girlfriend's mouth. My mom laughed but I just simply did not understand. Why would any guy pee in a girl's mouth? That was the most disgusting thing I ever heard. And 13 years later Jennifer killed herself. So what was it all for?

In fifth grade, after three months of pretending to enjoy hopscotch with the girls rather than kickball with the guys during recess, I finally had enough courage to tell Beth that maybe possibly I had real feelings for her. I can't remember what happened after that. Everyone was embarrassed. She was. I was. All of our friends were. Some running away occurred. But a few weeks later we started riding our bikes together after school. And then I started finding out certain things about myself that I never knew before but I would know all too well for years after.

- I was a jealous man. I mentioned to her that I thought Chris Herzog liked her. She giggled. I felt something then. Like someone played an awful D-minor chord on this guitar I never realized was built into the core of my chest.
- I was a stalker. She had a neighbor who was one year older than us. I could ride my bike past from two houses away and see through the woods if they were playing together. I rode

back and forth all day on any day we weren't bike riding together. He seemed like a cool guy. So I had no chance if he aimed his intentions in her direction (I was insecure was another thing I learned about myself but don't want to make it a bullet point).

- I hated snow. Once it started snowing, the game was over. I can't ride my bike in the snow. Which meant my ability to make my way over to her house was over. I cried the first day it snowed that fifth grade year.

- I was a manipulator. I became friends with all her friends. Even had mini-crushes on them. This way if she wasn't around I could find someone else to talk to about my feelings for her.

- I was a gossip. Once I recognized in myself the complicated chemical process that turns a piece of coal into a diamond in the heart, I thought I could recognize it in others. So when David Pakenham liked Joanne Arico, I wrote it down in my notebook, detailing all the subtle nuances in their interactions that I had observed. When Jimmy Biondo liked Lori Gumbinger, I wrote it down. I wrote down the names of so many potential 12-year-old couples that everyone was dying to see what was in my notebook and finally the teacher prevented me from bringing in that notebook ever again.

- I was a fighter. When Bryan Stryker was flirting with Beth one day, I jumped on him and hit him as hard as I could. Then he beat the total living crap out of me even though he was smaller and a year younger. That very day I quit taking piano lessons from his dad. And that was end of Beth and me bike riding together.

- I was nostalgic. That night, when I knew we'd never bike ride together (she said, specifically, "I never want to talk to you again") I thought of all the times we had spent together in the three weeks since I had confessed my love. My dad came into my room and asked why I was crying. "No reason," I said.

- She moved out of town a year or so later and to this day I have never seen her again. A few years ago, like scraping through the layers of an archaeological dig, I suddenly found myself Facebook friends with everyone I knew in fifth grade, including Beth. We started playing "Word Challenge" on Facebook. We would IM occasionally and share our respective sad stories at that time.

Now, the other day, via a status update on her wall, I was very happy to see she had just gotten remarried. She looked extremely happy in her new profile photo. Life is good.

I was certainly willing to pay $100 billion to see that photo.

HOW I SCREWED YASSER ARAFAT OUT OF $2 MILLION

I needed to make one hundred million dollars pretty fast. You know how it is. There are bills to pay. There are things you want to do in life. I wanted, for instance, to work as a cashier in a bookstore. But with a twist. I would own the bookstore. I wanted to do a 90 second ad in the Super bowl which would just be me walking around for 90 seconds saying and doing nothing. People would argue afterwards, "he could've used that money for charity. How selfish!" But I wouldn't care. It was my money and I could do what I want with it. I would be teaching this grand lesson to all the people watching the Super bowl. I had no other specific desires about what I would do with one hundred million dollars. Just those two. But I knew more things would come.

At the time (1999) I had recently made money selling a company in the web services business. Among other things, my company made the website for the movie, "The Matrix". I knew I was Neo but I wouldn't be able to take the red pill until I had my first hundred million. That was the pill that would let me be a real person. The pill that would allow me to be fully alive.

So I came up with an idea. It was a catchphrase and I would use it many times over the next six months. "First there was the wireLINE internet. Then there was the wireLESS internet. Which would be ten times bigger."

Those three sentences (or maybe its one if you use commas)

were my path to $100 million. Here's what you do then once you have your catchphrase. I had a business partner who wasn't shy. So he called up 20 companies in the wireless software business and said, "We want to buy your company." We had no money to buy anybody but if you ever let that slow you down you might as well run around naked in a football stadium with 60,000 people watching you.

One company responded. A company called "MobileLogic" out of Denver. They flew in and we took them out to breakfast at the Royalton Hotel on 44th Street. Its a fancy breakfast place. The sort of place Rupert Murdoch orders the pancakes, chews it up, spits it out without swallowing, and then orders granola to be healthy.

We're all sitting around a table. "Its fortunate that you called," the CEO of MobileLogic said to us. "Since Ericsson just offered us seventeen million and we're thinking of taking it." "Why would you take that," I said. "We'll offer you twenty million, half cash, half stock. That stock alone will be worth one hundred million or more once we go public. We have five other companies we'll buy after you. You'll be President of a major company thats going public, pronto. Ericsson is the old generation. Be apart of something new and exciting."

I love the pancakes at the Royalton. They whip the eggs into the batter. Its fluffy and delicious. And the bacon is thick and the bacon juices spill into your mouth as you bite into it. Life was good. Jerry Levin might very well have been at the table next to us buying AOL right in front of our eyes. That's how good life was then.

They took our offer. We quickly wrote up a binding LOI that they signed. We negotiated their salaries, their options, their earnout, everything. Now we needed to pay them twenty million dollars. We knew we could pay half the twenty in stock. So that was easy. That was a piece of paper. Now we had to come up with the other ten.

No problem. Because suddenly I had a real asset. I had a binding LOI for a company with $5-10mm in revenues (despite my propensity to remember every detail of my childhood, I can't remember how much in revenues this company I was buying in 1999 had). There were companies going public then with zero dollars in revenues that were now worth over a hundred trillion dollars.

So, with some partners who were excellent middlemen I started going to potential investors. Mark Patterson, who was then vice chairman of CSFB and is now the head of multi-billion dollar hedge fund Maitlin-Patterson set up a conference call with a few small investors. One call he set up was with Henry Kravis, Leo Hindery, Jim McMann (CEO of 1800-Flowers) and Dennis, something or other, who just sold a huge Irish telecom company and was worth a random billion or so. I gave a fifteen minute talk. I described my background and the company I had sold. Then I used my catchphrase (see above) and scoped out the opportunity ("10x the size of the wireline internet") and that was the call. Henry Kravis asked a question. I can't remember what it was now because all I kept thinking was "you were the barbarian at the gate and now I'm the barbarian."

Right after the call, Mark Patterson's phone started ringing. Mark told me, "Henry wants to wire five million right now." But we only took one from him. Too many other people wanted to invest. Everyone on that 15-minute conference call put in one million each.

At another meeting to raise money, I had to describe what we did. I wasn't even totally sure what MobileLogic did. We protected data that was in corporate databases but was being sent out to the salesforces through wireless devices that we set up. It was pretty solid. I said, "The data goes to the satellite and then comes down to our devices."

"I thought the data didn't go through satellites. Doesn't data go through cellular towers?" someone named Mamoon asked.

Uh-oh. That seemed to make more sense than satellites. "Sometimes," I answered.

And they put five million in. Frank Quattrone put money in. Sam Waksal, Allen & Co. CMGI. The list goes on. We were the hot investment for three seconds. One guy who had initially rejected us but then saw the list of investors called me at two in the morning and said, "please let me put in a million."

So we closed on thirty million dollars and bought our first company. Then we bought a second company. A consulting company called Katahdin. They had nothing to do with wireless but they had profits. We'd bury them in the IPO story but make use of their profits. Then we bought a third company. I can't even remember their name but they were a spinoff from MIT. Right away we were getting calls. Aether Systems wanted to buy us but we said no. They only wanted to pay fifty million for the company. A banker at CS First Boston told us he could get us seventy five million no problem. But we didn't even listen to him. In the elevator we laughed at him. What an old fool! We were going for an IPO.

Every bank came in with a PowerPoint and a team of young people to pitch us. Goldman, CSFB, Merrill, Lehman, etc. CSFB was the front-runner because Frank Quattrone was an investor but Merrill made a strong pitch. The pitch was funny. The top Merrill banker was there. He said to the associate on the deal, "John, walk them through the numbers." And John said, "uhh, my name is Roy". Two other things I remember from the pitch. The first was, "Henry Blodget will be the analyst on this deal. He loves wireless." Which made no sense to me since he was an Internet consumer analyst.

The other thing I remember was the back page of the presentation. The beautiful back page. The only page that mattered. It had what my net worth would be if we IPOed and the market valued us similar to Aether Systems. I would be worth something like nine hundred million dollars.

I knew exactly what bookstore I wanted to buy. It would be Shakespeare & Company on Broadway. None of the other employees would know that I would be the owner. And I would work just stacking books and being the guy at the cash register. My secret would give me infinite power.

I didn't know how to be CEO of this company. And because I didn't really know any of the employees of the companies we were buying I was feeling very shy. I would call my secretary before I arrived at work and ask her if anyone was in the hallway and could she please unlock my office door. Then I would hurry into the office and lock the door behind me.

Eventually they replaced me as CEO. Even later, when we had to raise up to another 70 million, they asked me to step off as a director on the board. At one point I arranged for a reverse merger to occur. We'd be public at at least at a hundred million dollar valuation. But the guy behind the reverse merger turned out to have a checkered past and had spent some time in jail in 1969 for either embezzlement or something to do with transporting fake diamonds. But thats another story.

None of this portrays me in a good light at all. Except for maybe the fact that I was a good salesman during the greatest bubble in world history. But it was decade ago and I don't mind what people think.

But I did learn several things that became incredibly important to me later:

A) If you have to raise thirty million to start your business, its probably not a good business (at least for me). All of my good businesses (businesses that I started that I eventually sold and made money on) started off profitable from day one and never raised a dime of money.

B) Most M&A transactions don't work. When you buy a company, its very hard to keep the owners of the old company incentivized. 90% of acquisitions don't work. Build your business. Don't buy it.

C) A lesson I learn repeatedly: traveling for business almost never generates more revenues. New York (and America) are big enough places to generate revenues. You should never travel. In the course of doing this business I traveled repeatedly to the west coast, Denver, England (to try and buy a company), Sweden (where Ericsson was based), Germany (Ericsson wanted me to show up at a conference for one day), Georgia, Florida, Boston, etc etc. Not a single meeting generated any revenues for the business but wasted hundreds of hours of my life.

D) Hiring smart people doesn't work if you aren't smart. Everything ultimately comes form the top down.

E) Spending a lot of money on branding and marketing materials is a waste of money for a startup. If you don't know who you are, no amount of money will create materials explaining who you are.

F) If you are going to raise thirty million for a business, then raise a hundred million if you can. Don't turn down Henry Kravis's five million. It doesn't matter how badly you get diluted. If you have to raise money, take in every dime you can.

G) MOST IMPORTANT: If you raise thirty million, spend none of it. Warren Buffett once said, "if you know a business will be around 20 years from now then it's probably a good investment." With thirty million we could've stayed in business for 20 years or more and eventually figured ourselves out. Instead, I spent forty million in the first month or so. I learned a lot, and over a hundred million was lost.

Eventually Vaultus (the name of the company. I think i forgot to mention it until now) was sold to Antenna Software. I made no money, as I rightfully shouldn't.

Four years later, I was on a train to Boston with my business partner. It was 5 in the morning and we were going up to visit a hedge fund we were invested in. He was reading Bloomberg magazine. "Holy shit," he said, waking me up. He showed me an article in the magazine. It was about Yasser Arafat, who had just died. Turns out he had a front corporation that was making various investments for him from the money he had somehow made off of the PLO. His largest (or second largest) investment was two million dollars he had put into a "New York company, Vaultus, Inc." I can tell you for a fact his estate lost that two million. So, as they say in Brooklyn, it was good for the Jews.

I'M GUILTY OF TORTURING WOMEN

I used to torture her on almost a daily basis. It was almost to the point where I can't forgive myself. I remember one sorry anguished moment where she was crying and begging me to stop but I couldn't because I'm an addict. Sometimes torturers can't help it. Whether its nature or nurture they feel the need to keep going at it.

I was 24 years old and I had just sent out my very first novel to about 20 publishers and 20 agents. I had misappropriated the copy machine in graduate school right before they kicked me out (cc: Merrick Furst, now a dean at Georgia Tech) so I could print up 50 or so copies of my novel. All of the publishers and all of the agents responded with a form letter rejection but I didn't know that yet. All I knew was that I had to write the second novel.

Within hours of starting the second novel I had doubts about the topic. Was it boring? I started asking her. We were walking in the street in Pittsburgh. Pittsburgh has no people in it so its ok to walk in the street at all times of the day or night. I kept asking her about who she thought the audience was for the novel. I was skeptical of all her answers but I knew, since I had already put two solid hours of hard work into this masterpiece, that I had to finish it no matter how long it took or what she said. Finally she said: "will you stop talking to me about King fucking David for one second?"

But I couldn't stop. For months and months that's all I talked about. I would write 1500 words in the morning, read novels for about four hours so I would stay in the flow, and then write about 1500 words at night. Any break I had I would talk to her about what I was writing.

She was working on her PhD in anthropology. What was her topic? I have no clue. We were a couple for three years. We lived together. Two of our bookcases were filled with her books and two with mine. I have no idea what she wrote her PhD on. Something about pregnant women in Sardinia. I think she's a lawyer now. Or a mother. Or a lawyer/mother.

I took a break once. There was a contest where you had to write a novel in one weekend. I did it. About 120 pages. It was called: "The Porn Novelist, The Romance Novelist, the Prostitute, and They're Lovers." Not having any experience with anything remotely related to the protagonists I can now say it is unreadable. Particularly since I just re-read it a few weeks ago.

Finally I finished my novel and I gave it to Sue K. to read. I would use her last name except she de-friended me on Facebook about two years ago and so maybe she wants her privacy.

I sat there while she read it. I didn't really move at all because its very important to read the facial reactions of the girl who you are going out with and living with who is reading your book. Like if she smirks a little I would need to know what line she was smirking about, why she was smirking, and whether or not she was faking her smirk.

About nine hours later she finished reading all 416 pages.

She closed the last page, and said, "That was fantastic. I really liked it." She said again, "I really liked it."

I asked her to describe to me how it ended. The final chapter that was like the code-breaker to the rest of the novel, without which the novel could not be understood. Because I was an artist.

She turned red. "It was great," she said.

"But ok, just tell me what happened in the last chapter."

"I'm tired," she said. She had been sitting there for nine hours. I forget now if I fed her at all during this time.

"Just tell me what happened in the last chapter. How can you say it was great and not know what happened in the last chapter?" She started to cry. And so I began to torture her because she was deliberately ruining my entire life. I feel bad now. She's a respected lawyer/mother/PhD somewhere in the United States.

"Please," she said, "I read it but I'm tired right now. I just can't remember this second. I'm on the spot."

No, I said. I'M ON THE SPOT! Because you just read my novel and now we need to have a discussion about it.

A few years after we had broken up, we were still friends. We would talk on the phone every few months. Old friends who lived in distant cities used to do that in the late 20th century. She was about to get married to the guy she met after me.

"He makes toys," she said, "and works from home in a workshop he set up." That sounds neat, I said, he must be good with his hands. "Oh yes," she said, and giggled, "he's very good with his hands." And, with just those words, she got her revenge.

HOW TO SUCCEED IN LA
WITHOUT REALLY TRYING

She asked me if she could play. I was in a bar in a hotel in LA going over a game on a portable chessboard while waiting for Steve to arrive so we could go out for dinner. This woman sat down about two seats from me, looked over, and then challenged me to a game.

It was almost surreal because nothing like that had ever happened to me before. It was like a scene from a chess movie only nobody would ever make a movie about chess. How could I refuse? So we started the first few moves and she wasn't awful. She told me her last boyfriend was Benecio del Toro but now he wasn't calling her back. And now she was playing chess with me. The only reason I was staying at this hotel, "The Bel Age", was because that's where the TV show Beverly Hills 90210 had their prom.

Steve finally arrived and I introduced them. I want to think she seemed sad to see me leave.

We left. I was thinking I was pretty cool at that moment. Steve was like, "what the fuck!? That was a high end prostitute!"

"No way," I said, "she played chess." Somehow all the circuitry in my brain was fried. Everything was on fire.

"Man," he said, "she was a call girl. The last time I was in this hotel I saw [owner of now defunct record store chain] with prostitutes all over him. She was a call girl."

Maybe it was the thought that she was "high end" made me feel a little better about it? I don't know.

Steve and I went to dinner where we met up with a guy who had just gotten out of jail. Steve and I were tiny Jews in LA. This guy was the opposite of that. He was the size of three bathroom stalls put together. He said over dinner, "when [jailed famous hip hop mogul] gets out of jail, Snoop better be in hiding. I give him 30 days before Snoop is dead." As we were walking out of dinner, he said to me, "I really like what you do. Can I stop by and hang out in your office next time I'm in New York?"

What can you say to that?

On the way back to the hotel I ask Steve if he's going to pay his bills anytime soon. His company owed me $80k. I had a payroll of 40 people I had to make. Steve was in charge of Internet stuff for [famous record label]. "Why are you always asking me that?" Steve said, "Don't you trust me? And your guy Adrian was threatening my secretary today. Tell him to back the fuck off or I'll never fucking pay you." Now I had to apologize because I never did business back then with a contract so I had nobody to sue. It was all "relationships".

We stopped off at a bar where the owner of Steve's record label was hanging out in a booth with two beautiful girls. He was a billionaire known for having multiple women around all the time. Steve introduced us and said to him, "you guys would get along. James plays chess." And the guy said, "Oh yeah? I just sponsored the World Chess Championship with Kasparov" but then turned away and started kissing one of the girls.

At the bar was [famous comedian] whose tv show I had just done the website for. I was feeling shy but Steve laughed and encouraged me to go over and introduce myself. I went over to him and said, "Hey, sorry for interrupting but I'm a big fan. I just wanted to mention that I just did your website for your TV show." He looked at me, squinted for a second or two and said, very very slowly, "who. are. you.?" and then everyone around him laughed.

The next day I went over to UTA, the big talent agency that represented, among others, Jim Carrey. "We love your stuff," they said, "we want to do something big with Jim Carrey. It has to be really really big." I threw out some ideas. "We LOVE that. Lets do it!" One guy said, "you should come with us to this party tonight."

But I was unsure if I had other plans. An hour later, when my other plans canceled I called one of them and said, "hey, I can go to that party," and he said, "oh, we made other plans but we LOVED your stuff. Call us next time you are in town and we'll do something." I never spoke to him again despite repeated calls when I got back to New York.

For one thing, I wear sweaters. And I don't drive. People in LA don't get either of those things. I tend to look different and stand out because I'm walking on the side of the road a lot.

I had breakfast the next morning with a guy who invented the kind of pen where it changes according to how your fingers press it. He was in his late 50s but was tan and fit. He wanted to make a website to sell his pens. He ordered pancakes and french toast but had only one bite of each. "I like to test things," he said, "for my restaurant. You should stop by." I had done a website once for a movie he produced. Headless Body In Topless Bar. "I lost a half million on that movie. You know what that's like?" I said no.

He opened up his cellphone. "This is technology. This is where its going." He had a speaker on the cellphone and called someone. A sleepy sounding woman answered, "Hello?" "Hello, baby," he said, "Just showing my new friend this new technology." Then he snapped it shut. "I don't like you," he said to me. "You didn't comb your hair before you came to meet me and you're disheveled. You should clean up a little if you want to do business with me."

Later that day I had lunch with a friend of mine [see The Girl Whose Name Was a Curse] who had moved to LA a year earlier. She was now a Pilates instructor for [famous female comedian]. "I love it here," she said. "Its so much healthier." I felt bad it never worked out with us (and I never had a chance) but she was married now and she really did look happy and healthy.

Later that night I took the red eye home. I can never sleep in planes so I try to read but I'm too tired and end up in this weird stupor while everyone sleeps in the dark around me. When I landed I went straight into the office. It was early and the sun was just creeping out. I could see the smoke from my breath in the cold air when I got into the cab. My sister was already at the office when I got there. "Hey!" she said, "how was LA?"

It was awesome.

IMAGINE YOU ARE TEN YEARS OLD

Imagine you are a nine-year-old girl. Imagine how excited you are because tomorrow you are going to turn ten. Think back to how you were feeling then. What would it be like to be two digits old instead of one?

You can't even imagine. Will it feel different than being nine? You will never be single digits again. You know this means the entire world will be different but you can't even imagine what will be different about it. You try to remember your first memory but it's hidden by clouds and you can't see it.

Imagine your parents are divorced. You remember them arguing all the time. You remember when you were six, asking them at your older sister's scared prompting, if they were going to get divorced. You tiptoe into the kitchen where they are arguing, where they ignore you because of their yelling even though they know you are there. They are screaming. They are twice as large as you. You want to ask them a question. Imagine saying: "excuse me".

Imagine saying, "Josie wants to know if you two are staying

together." And they come over to you and hug you and you don't know if that's an answer or not. You don't know what you will say to your older sister who is upstairs waiting for you. You don't know whether or not to be scared.

You remember your father getting so angry the police had to come. You remember them walking him out to their car in the middle of the night. You remember being scared. Then the next morning, the sun just barely up, you, your mother and your sister going out into the middle of nowhere and picking him up at a motel. You remember him getting into the car and not saying anything. Imagine the red and orange blurs of the sunrise, obliterating the night that just happened. Nobody says anything. Nobody ever brought it up ever again.

Imagine your father not coming home one day. "He's working busy in the city again," you think, even when he doesn't show up for Thanksgiving. Even when nobody says anything to you.

Imagine every two weeks driving seventy miles into New York with your mother so you can be dropped off with your father. Imagine your father taking you and your sister to ping pong, pool, bowling, museums, rock climbing, going ice skating, going to magic shows, eating out three times a day, playing games, eating more, and finally you are exhausted and are driven home late Sunday night before school the next day. You are sad because you are so exhausted. There was no break. You are too exhausted. You are sad because why isn't your father driving home with you?

Imagine your father and mother finally telling you they are getting divorced a few months later. You cry because you don't want to be "one of them". You think of the other kids in school whose parents are divorced. Now you are in that club. You don't want to be. You cry.

Imagine a year later, your father moving back into the town you live. You are so happy. Maybe, you think, you will all be one big happy family again. You remember when everyone is together and he is always making jokes. But you remember the fighting. You remember him throwing things. You remember the police coming. You were scared. But now he's back in town. You have a bedroom in his house. You imagine what it's going to look like. You're excited about the spiral staircase he tells you is in his house.

He drives you and your older sister to his new house for the first time. On the way there he pulls over. He says to you there is also a woman at the house and that he's in love with the woman and he's going to marry her. You start to cry. "What?" you remember saying. You try to picture what she looks like.

But then he says, "She has met you girls before and she will love you girls very much." And you say, "Wait? Who is she?"

And you remember that your daddy let her watch you a few times when you were in the city and he had to go off to a meeting. And you remember liking her and that maybe this won't be so bad. But you also, deep down, miss the idea that it won't be one big happy family like it once was.

Imagine you're about to turn ten the next day and in fifteen minutes you have to go to school. You and your mother park by the river to watch it flow by. You have a few spare minutes each day before school after your older sister is dropped off. Your mother and you take a walk by the river.

Imagine then your father jogging up to the car. He lives right next to the river. He's got a bag. His new wife is with him. She's carrying a bag. The bags have all your birthday presents in them. It's everything you wanted. They both hug you. You're smiling. You're happy to see both of them. You want to open up all the bags and boxes and presents. Before they got there you were reading a book that was a fictionalized version of the young Anastasia. But now all you can think about are your new presents.

Your father and his wife kiss you. You are smiling from end to end. "It's not my birthday yet", you say. But tomorrow you will be double-digits. Your father says, "Next year we will turn back the clock and you will be nine again. No more of this double-digit stuff."

You look at your mom and you look at Claudia. Daddy is being crazy again. You smile. Your step-mom takes out the doll she got. "Isn't she pretty?" You say, "yes." You are very happy. Sometimes things don't work out just right. But sometimes you can be happy anyway. There's a doll. There are pencils. There are accessories. There's going to be a sleepover, and a brunch, and then your daddy is going to take you out for dinner. It's a weekend of celebration for your birthday

Imagine you are back in the car. Your daddy and step-mom are running in the cold back to their house where you now have a room you share with your sister. They've left the presents behind that you can look at in the fifteen minutes before school begins. You are smiling from cheek to cheek, freckles spread across your face like meaning on a tarot card. You think of the weekend ahead

Tomorrow you will go from nine years old to ten years old. And for the rest of your life you will be double-digits. Will you see the other side of that? Will you see three digits? You look at your new doll. Nothing will ever go wrong in the world again.

Imagine you are going to be ten years old tomorrow. Double digits for the first time. You already miss the single digits. You won't be a baby again. With no worries. You can't imagine what double digits will be like. Imagine that you are my daughter and it seems like nothing will be the same ever again.

WHEN I WAS COMPLETELY HUMILIATED BY YOGA

I woke up yesterday to the sounds of a woman throwing up for fifteen straight minutes. It might've been the woman who lives next door. Vomiting seems to come with the territory in India. And vomiting is not one consistent sound. If someone says to you, "I just heard a note from a piano", you'd have to ask: "Was it a C sharp? Was it from the high end of the piano or the deep end? Was it loud, soft, long, staccato? For fifteen minutes this woman played for me a complete symphony. The deepest recesses of her throat were the most beautiful instruments I had ever heard.

Which brings me to yoga. I'm not an athlete (but I was a mathlete in school). I'm not flexible, pliable, and my back muscles aren't ripped and shredded. I've never stood in my head. And I get embarrassed when I hear people chant for religious reasons. So, practicing yoga in India becomes a story of humiliation, weakness, disappointment, and frustration for me. And I'm only on my second class here. Some of the things hard for me so far:

1. **Worst in class.** In class, I'm the first one who was forced to stop. There are about 100 people at my level (beginner). The moves start off fairly easy, and then get harder and harder. Saraswati, the daughter of Pattabhi Jois, who started Ashtanga Yoga, is leading the class. About 45 minutes in she looks over at me. I'm drenched in sweat. Everything hurts. The other people in the class are shining like gods, their sweat illuminating the etches of their brilliant muscles. I smell like gutter. Saraswati looks over at me, "you stop now." So I'm the first to stop.

2. **Everyone looks at me.** I have to stay until the end of the class because we all do the closing moves together. So I'm sitting there not sure what to do. I'm in the back of the class. There's one move where everyone twists around. When I say "twist around" its almost like a science fiction movie where the aliens twist around their waist 360 degrees in order to make sure there's no danger. So everyone is twisting around in this impossible position, looking straight at me, the one guy in the back of the room not doing the move. Is this fair? Do I look back at them? Should I pretend I'm the teacher and they are all looking back at me for approval? Instead, I look down and act like I'm meditating.

3. **The men in the class are perfect.** I'm the only guy in the class who keeps my shirt on. Which is why I mention above I smell like gutter. Its worse than that though. I smell like something is dead in the walls of your house. The other guys take their shirts off. They have tattoos of dragons on their backs and crawling up their arms. They have muscles in places called tibias, femurs, and psoas. Parts of the body I never heard of. Like when you suddenly look at a map of the world and realize for the first time that Africa is broken

up into many tiny countries that you never knew existed and most likely will never visit.

4. **My secret revealed.** There was a move where both teaching assistants and Saraswati had to come over and put me in position. I knew that they knew my secret then. That I was just pretending to be here. One woman pushing my back down. The other woman whispering urgently, relax your arm and stretch it out this way. Saraswati saying, "leg wants go here!" My leg had never taken directions before. It never wanted anything before. I was praying at the time, "just let the fingers from my left hand clasp the fingers from my right hand behind me so they could leave."

5. **Yoga vision.** Today I was waiting outside for Claudia to finish her class. Today was my "rest day". The advanced class was waiting to go in so there were about 40 advanced level students and me waiting outside. They all looked at me when I showed up. I was the special guest. Yoga supposedly makes your eyes shine brighter. This is what Claudia tells me. All of the advanced students looked at me with their x-ray vision. Their heat vision. I melted into the dust.

6. **Sanskrit.** At breakfast at a local restaurant there were no Indians. Only yoga students still glistening from the sweat of their practice. Everyone was comparing notes on their class. "I had trouble with the full stretch on Utthita Hasta Padangusthasana". "I finally got past Ardha Baddha Padma Paschimottanasana". It seemed like everyone was fluent in some sort of yoga-ized Sanskrit. They all ordered things like granola. I had two orders of pancakes with bananas inside. Mmmm. It was good.

7. **Chanting.** At the beginning of class there's a chant. It starts off with a big "Ommmm". I can handle that. But then it goes into something else that I can't understand. Everyone else

is doing the chant. For some reason I blush and I try to hum along with it but then blush more because why am I even humming?

8. **Earnestness.** People say things like, "its good its crowded here. More people in the world are doing yoga." They are earnest about it and everyone is agreeing. I'm not sure how to respond. Maybe, "I feel like world peace might be right around the corner." Or, "If only everyone had a fully developed tibia muscle less people might get divorced."

9. **Coconuts.** After practice on the first day I was sweating so much I thought I would have no more water left in my body. "Drink coconut juice," Claudia said to me and there was a guy cutting coconuts right outside the class. "It will give you electrolytes." All of the other students were outside drinking coconut juice already. They knew the drill. We're monkeys from a million generations ago and we need our coconuts so we can mate and have children. But I don't like coconut juice so we leave the other students there, all filling up with electrolytes so they can laugh and flirt once again.

10. **Cold Shower.** After the first class I went home to take a shower. But I'm not quite used to the smell of the water here yet. I am saying this very politely. And I couldn't figure out how to get hot water. So I took a freezing cold shower and couldn't get the soap off my skin. So for the rest of the day I was scratching all over like a wild animal, leaving scratch marks everywhere, when the soap dried into my skin and mixed with the general grime and dust outside.

Its day four and I love every minute of my trip here. Tomorrow is my third class.

MY NAME IS JAMES A AND I'M AN ALCOHOLIC

It was my first meeting of Alcoholics Anonymous. I went to the meeting at that church at the corner of Wall Street and Broadway. I think it's the oldest church in the country. Or the city. Or the "oldest" "something of "somewhere". We were in the basement and donuts were served. There were about six rows of seats and a dozen or so people were randomly spaced out on them, as if none of us could get too close to each other.

We went up and down the rows introducing ourselves. When it came to me I wasn't sure what to say. I had never been to a meeting before so I more or less copied everyone else. "My name is James and this is my first day of no alcohol." At that, everyone gave a little bit of a clap. "Welcome, James". The leader of the meeting said.

The thing is, I wasn't an alcoholic. I didn't drink at all. And I really didn't want to go to this particular meeting. To make it even worse, an astrologer had told me to go to a 12 step meeting of Business Owners Debtors Anonymous (BODA). But there were no BODA meetings that day so she said, "go to an AA meeting instead. They are all the same." But they weren't all the same. What are you supposed to say if you are not an alcoholic and now it's your turn to speak? I felt like a secret agent behind the Iron Curtain. But I liked the clapping. I felt some pleasure at being so welcomed. But I also felt a little guilty and when the meeting was over I ran away.

A few weeks later I found a BODA meeting to go to at a church on 31st and 7th. Everyone was sitting around in a circle. I liked that. I felt we could all go around in a circle telling stories about ourselves. Like Show-n-Tell in 1st grade. I felt like my show-n-tell would be better than anyone else's. I was there for ego purposes. I wanted all of the other kids in the circle to love me. The truth of the matter even here, though, was that I was neither a business owner at this time, nor a debtor. But here I was, at business owner's debtor's anonymous. I also was under the delusion that all of these people needed my help. That I had something to teach them.

People started telling their stories. One woman I remember said: "The good thing is that since I've been going to these meetings is that I don't need as much money."

What!?

At the time, I didn't necessarily think that was such a good thing. I felt like she was just fooling herself. Of course she needed a billion dollars. She was being hypnotized into settling for less. I didn't think she was a "loser" but maybe I was thinking only one level higher than that.

There was one real pretty girl in the BODA meeting. I aimed my story at her. I told the whole thing. I expected intense clapping and whistling at the end but there was none of that and people just went on to the next person. When it was the pretty girl's turn she talked about how she was in intense debt, she didn't like her employer, but she had done something 'so horribly shameful [she] couldn't even admit it in BODA'.

We were all sort of silent then. I'm sure all of us were thinking the same thing. She was wearing a short skirt. What could she have done? I was insanely turned on by her. But then the group went onto the next person.

I can't remember anything else about the meeting. After the meeting was over, the pretty girl disappeared. People were milling around talking but nobody really talked to me at all so I left.

Outside I had one of the weirdest coincidences for me ever. About two years earlier I had invested $300,000 in a company called (don't laugh) gooey.com. They were an Israeli company and I ended up on the board of directors of the company. Try not to go on the board of directors of an Israeli company. By the time the experience was over it was so bad I thought I was even going to have to sue myself.

They had software that would turn web pages into chat rooms. So if I had the gooey software downloaded and you did also and we were both on the same web page then we would be able to see each other via the software and start chatting. I thought this was the "new thing" in instant messaging. I put in $300,000 and I got a bunch of other people to put in about $700,000. Two years later gooey.com declared bankruptcy. And about three months after that I found myself in my first AA meeting.

So right after I left the BODA meeting there was a homeless guy sitting about a half block from the church. I'm not exaggerating when I say he was lying in his own urine. I'm not exaggerating when I say, coming out of this BODA meeting where I just described, among other things, losing $300,000 on this company, this homeless man lying in his urine was wearing a gooey.com t-shirt. The shirt had a very distinctive logo and colors. I went right up to the guy to make sure I was seeing it correctly.

It was definitely the gooey shirt. I felt like God was sending me a message. I still don't know what to make of the coincidence. I had never even seen anyone other than myself wearing the t-shirt before. I left the man a $20 dollar bill. I don't think he noticed. [As a side note, every single thing I write in this here is dead true. Please don't even write in the reviews that this story is not true. Although if I must be honest I don't remember if it was a $20 dollar bill or a ten dollar bill I left with the guy but I'm guessing the higher.]

About a year earlier Gooey had an offer to be acquired for about $100 million from Star Media, the Latin American portal company. I would've made about $4 million on the deal. This was the peak of the bubble. I was begging the company to take the offer. I arranged for the deal to be entirely hedged with a collar put on by Morgan Stanley (dba Justin Weil, "the mad collarer") the second the deal closed so the Star Media stock would be as good as cash.

I visited with the top guys in the company. They were in a random apartment one of them had rented on the west side. At the time their software had about a million downloads but no revenues. "We don't want Star Media!" they told me. "We're Gooey! We want someone prestigious like Yahoo!" Israelis playing video games while discussing $100 million acquisitions always talk with exclamation points. Otherwise I wouldn't be so liberal in their use. So that deal went down the toilet. As did another potential deal gooey had with the company that is now SIGA Technologies for $150 million. A year later they were bankrupt.

I barely remember the AA meeting, and I only feel mild disappointment now when thinking about what could've been with a Star Media acquisition. Things have worked out for the best in my life without that $4 million I would've made on the deal. Thank god they didn't take it. And 12 years later I even managed to convince myself to invest in another Israeli company. I got over my hatred of Israeli entrepreneurs. I love them now. And I relish coincidences. The homeless guy in the Gooey tshirt can only be topped if I tell you it was also raining outside, which it was, and I had no umbrella, which I didn't, so I was completely soaked, staring at my $300,000 literally down the drain in a pool of urine, and I was thoroughly depressed.

But not because of this homeless guy.

I knew that all the coincidences in the world were not going to make my dream that evening come true. Because the pretty girl who sat across from me in the BODA meeting had just confessed in the meeting to doing "the most shameful thing I had ever done".

And in my imagination I saw us twenty years later, all our worries behind us, smiling into each other's faces in our cozy house with a fireplace and maybe some kids running around. And maybe right when she was about to drift off into blissful sleep that night twenty years in the future she would finally whisper into my ear, and I would barely be able to hear her – she would finally tell me the shameful secret she had been holding back from me after all of these years.

MY LAWYER IS DEAD

About two years ago I met with a lawyer about an SEC issue I was having. The details are not important. He was a little overweight, bushy mustache, a plaid sort of suit that didn't match up right, he had driven in two hours from Long Island. I had arranged a fancy place, thinking that if he thought I could be a big client he would make the two hour drive and give me a free consultation. Which he did.

Most of the meeting he kept complaining about how "lousy" it was to be a lawyer. He was complaining about his kids. His wife. The two-hour commute. His clients. How many of his clients were total criminals. How the government was criminal. "But," he says: "This is what I do. It's too late for me to do anything else." When we were all leaving we stopped by the bathroom. He came out of the stall, didn't stop to wash his hands, yelled out, "see you later," and went on his way.

Over the next two years I would run into him occasionally. One guy called him "my dear friend" and the "smartest lawyer I know". Another group that worked on the 59th floor of 40 Wall Street laughed hysterically when I said that K. said he was the best lawyer in the sector. They even called another lawyer on the speakerphone and said, "hey, guess what K. said he was the expert at." And everyone laughed.

We all, coincidentally knew K and over the 20 or so years K had been in business in the lowest, shadiest, stinkiest part of Wall Street, he had demonstrated a flare for...well, nothing really.

Yesterday K, 49 years old, died of a heart attack.

He just gave up. I don't care about the technical details of heart disease. He clearly didn't need to die and could've done stuff to avoid it.

But he gave up. He was tired of it all.

Tired starts when you can't get up in the morning. When you can't look your wife in the face and say good morning but there's no way to avoid it day after day. When you have kids that you just don't know how to support and you start losing the ability to care. When you have clients and you think, "ugh, not another f-ing one of these." When you have to drive two hours to meet some shitty guy who you know is going to just get a free consultation out of you but you do it anyway.

Day after day. No day different. Maybe you had other dreams. but maybe you didn't. Everyone told you that being a lawyer would make you a lot of money, would bring you safety. Safety that would protect you to death. But who are you going to make happy today? Your mother, because you are alive, her little baby? Your wife? Your kids? Your customers? The ones who appreciate your art? When will it finally matter?

You have a drink at the bar before going home. Maybe two or three. You watch sports but you forget which team is which. You want to watch sports with your kids but they don't care. You want to watch with friends on a Sunday with some beers but you have no friends.

You're tired. And bit by bit you see a glimpse of something

but you can't tell what it is. It's not the famous final last words of Steve "oh wow" Jobs. Its a feeling in the heart. A feeling of pressure. Something has become disconnected but only you know it. Something has finally given you the choice. You push at it. You sense what it is. You eat a little more. Drink a little more. Sometimes you can't move but then you do because you know you are pushing it. You're too tired when you wake up. Not another f-ing day. But you get up because you know what you are pushing at.

Every day, a tiny bit, you finally realize deep down you have a choice. You push at it. You press the button. You visit your clients again but deep down you know you have a secret that they don't know. You experience sudden acts of kindness and the people around you are surprised. "He was a good man," they said to me later. Because you knew the Secret that they didn't know.

And one day you wake up and everything feels light again. You don't feel surprised about how happy you feel. It's natural. There are no worries. No clients. No bank accounts. No bathroom stalls. You jump out of bed. The window is open and you fly out. You skim through the trees and laugh. You fly to the moon and back. You forget who your clients were. You forget what your name was. You forget the irregularities of the nuances in SEC law. You forget everything. You've shed your body a million years ago and you're no longer tired.

You were a shitty lawyer. And now you're not.

I Want My Kids to Be Drug Addicts

Lynn, our child's babysitter, was a drug addict and her doctor told her that her brain scan was the same as that of an 80 year old man's who had multiple strokes. Lynn was afraid to tell us she needed to take a few days off from watching Josie so she could go on Oprah to talk about her brain scan, drugs, sex, and whatever else. She was worried we would fire her and she had neglected to tell us some things when she was hired to babysit our one year old.

Lynn was great with Josie and we considered her part of the family. Mollie was coming along soon and Lynn would be babysitter for both kids.

She decided to tell us: she had been addicted to the drug, Ecstasy. She had been hospitalized. Her before and after brain scans were going to be on Oprah and it would be a mess to watch. And, finally, she would be sitting on the couch with Oprah and they would chat about it and reveal all. Lynn felt we should know all of this stuff before any of our neighbors told us.

She was coming out of the subway the day she decided to tell us when the subway got bombed by terrorists. Not only the subway but the two buildings, the World Trade Center, that were on top of the subway.

So everything got delayed.

A week or so later she told us and then a week or so after that she was on Oprah. Here's her brain scan:

Lynn chose herself to succeed. Nobody was going to give it to her. Her father was missing in action. She became an addict. She was a college drop-out. And things went from bad to worse when she had a mental collapse and found herself hospitalized.

When she got out of the hospital she became Josie's babysitter. She also decided she was going to use her experiences to help people.

She wrote to MTV and went on one of their shows to describe what happened to her. Oprah saw the show and then wanted Lynn on the Oprah Show. After Oprah, Lynn put together a book proposal about her addiction.

It wasn't the regular twelve step thing. "You have to love your addiction," she told me. "You have to learn to accept it and learn to accept what it is inside of you that caused you the pain that leapt into that addiction. Only then can you deal with it. Everything is about acceptance." The other day she told me, "We often hide the good, the pretty, the successful inside ourselves from the bad, the failure, the ugly. They have to unify else we get fragmented inside ourselves and we can't accept who we are."

She got a book deal. A great one. She was still Josie and Mollie's babysitter for another 18 months. But then unfortunately she quit. She moved to California and finished the book. Probably a better choice for her then watching two little kids. I highly recommend the book.

She didn't stop with the book. A vision expands and expands until it fills up your entire universe. You can't stop it. There are no frontiers to passion.

She started writing to schools and prisons and anywhere else she could think of to speak about addiction. She began traveling around the country giving talks. She was making a living.

During this time I often got two questions from people who knew the story:

"Didn't you mind that a drug addict was your daughter's babysitter?" Of course not. In fact, we paid her more when she asked for it. Everyone goes through adversity in their lives. Being honest about the pain inside and not trying to run from it or even suppress it is the key to much success. I can say that since I've started writing in my blog for instance, unbelievable opportunities have dropped down on me.

The other question, the more annoying one, came from close relatives who asked: "If a drug addict can get a book deal, don't you think I should be able to get a book deal?" And my answer: of course not. You have nothing to write about. Then they say, "So you're saying I should be a drug addict." I don't know what I'm saying. I never really know what I'm saying so forgive me.

Lynn moved to California, her book came out, and she became a successful speaker making thousands per talk and speaking all over the country.

I had an investor, Dave, who was single. He lived in California also. He liked two things: surfing and investing. I introduced him to Lynn. On their first date they both called me afterwards and said they had a great time. On their second date, Dave was wearing a heavy backpack when he showed up at her house. Lynn said, "why are you wearing a backpack?" And Dave said, "because I'm moving in." And he moved in for many years and whenever they could afford it they traveled all over the world.

For awhile they even stayed in an abandoned home that I unfortunately owned until it was recently sold.

Then they broke up. "Traveling is your first love," Lynn told Dave. "And I can't be in second place." She wrote down all the things she wanted in life. Among them, one of the things she wrote was that she wanted a house with a treehouse.

A year after that Lynn was married, pregnant, owned a beautiful house in LA. In the back, the house had a treehouse. Claudia and I visited a few days ago. I'm afraid of heights but I even went up there to look around at the LA horizon.

But she still didn't stop. Again, passion has no frontiers. It fills up every emptiness and delivers value to everyone around you.

"Try these," Lynn said, and gave us some cupcakes made by the business she and her sister were starting. The cupcakes are gluten free and the brand is called "Whisk". The cupcakes were unbelievable and I normally hate gluten-free. I think I ate the whole box. Lynn's new husband, Brady, is a talent manager and is able to help her get the cupcakes in the hands of celebrities. They all love the cupcakes. Here's an example:

Lynn had dropped out of college when she was younger. "I wasn't learning anything," she said. Her dad was never a help to her. She became a drug addict. She had been hospitalized and close to death because of it.

Since then she's spoken to and helped tens of thousands of kids about drug addiction, written a book, been on Oprah, gotten thousands of letters from kids who were grateful for her, married the man of her dreams and moved into the house of her dreams and now is creating a very successful gluten-free baking company. She has more energy than anyone I know. Coming out of an addiction (a negative passion) can unleash all the positive passions. I hope Josie and Mollie turn out just like her.

I Want to Be Like Google When I Grow Up

Dear Google, I sort of want to have sex with you. Or I want you to be my father. Or my best friend. I don't know, I feel so nervous writing this letter. I hope you write back but you can't because you're God and God has to care for all of Her People and not just one tiny little person like me.

Dear Google,

The other day I wanted to learn about "Vincent Van Gogh". I saw a book in the bookstore but it looked boring and it was around 1000 pages. Who would read such a book?

But when I was thumbing through it I saw how he was trying to become friends with other artists and how he was trying to organize exhibitions of other artists. It was almost like he was trying to build his TRIBE, which is a modern word to describe a group with similar interests who try to help each other.

Van Gogh had the right idea. I wanted to read more about it but the book looked too boring. I also wanted to read about his ear.

So I asked you instead, Google. And you instantly replied to me.

First off, thanks for not calling me "stupid". I had spelled "Vincent" as "Vincenet". A lot of people would've yelled at me and said, "you fucking idiot. Don't you ever proofread what your write?" I do proof read but I'm not very good at it. I'm an idiot and I appreciate you not calling me out on that.

You politely said, "Showing results for Vincent Van Gogh". Very subtle, Google. Point noted. And you showed me 14,700,000 results.

WOW! And in your omniscience you showed me all the results of those 14 million that you thought were the most relevant.

There's also something unsaid in what you wrote back to me, Google.

Without saying it, you basically told me, "I, Google, know nothing about Vincent Van Gogh. But here are 14 million other places you can go and I've taken the time to read through all of them very quickly and tell you the ones I think are best."

You didn't even ask me to pay, or to come back again, or to say hello to anyone. You know nothing and aren't afraid to admit it. And you weren't afraid of hoarding the information. You just gave it to me.

I love you.

—m—

Dear Google,

I've been thinking more about that "Vincenet" (haha. That's an inside joke we now have, Google.) Van Gogh situation.

Here's what I'm learning from it. You are worth $200 billion so it's worth taking lessons from you on how to be a God among people.

A) **Be the source.** It seems like you don't really know anything. But you freely give to people advice on where they can go to get their answers. I want to be the source. If you're the source, you never have to worry about people coming back to you. They will. You give ideas, suggestions, pointers to information.

Most people are afraid to be the source. It's like when I used to be in the web design business a long time ago. People would ask me about my competitors. i'd be afraid to recommend them because then maybe people wouldn't love me as much. But people love you google, even though you constantly send them away.

It's like people love you because you are unavailable to them emotionally. You keep trying to get them to love others.

B) You're really honest. You told me what websites I should go to for "rentals in Encinitas" but you also told me which of the sites you were recommending paid you. So you had a conflict of interest. When I'm in the doctor's audience and he prescribes a medicine or sends me to another specialist I never have any idea if there is some other payment going back and forth between them. Thanks Google, for the honesty.

C) I need to freely give all of my ideas without thinking of any benefit to myself.

D) I need to freely introduce people each other without always inserting myself in the middle so I get some of the pie that is being divided. There is no pie. That's just me feeling non-abundant. You don't have a scarcity complex, Google, but I do.

E) I don't need to worry if people will come back to me. If I love everyone, like you do Google, then people will return.

F) I need to always be honest.

G) I have to make sure to not make people feel stupid.

H) It's ok to admit I don't know something. I notice you don't really have any opinions, Google. I like that. Instead, you are free with your information regardless of who talks to you and what they talk to you about. I'm tired of opinions anyway. Who ever wins in an argument over opinions? Both people lose.

I) **I should never hoard.** I told Claudia the other day I was having trouble coming up with ideas to write about. I also told her I had 200 posts in my "Drafts" folder that I wasn't releasing yet. She said "You're hoarding!" She said, "You won't have new ideas until you stop the hoarding." She's right. I should learn from you, Dear Google, because you don't hoard. You just give and you know you'll have more and more to give.

J) **You're cool.** If you "google", "Sergey Brin" and "glasses" and "NYC subway" there is a picture of Sergey Brin on the NYC subway wearing Google Glasses. He looks really cool. I want to be just like your high priest.

—ᴡ—

Dear Google, I just got the following email and it made me think of you:

"Hi James, I'm off for my new adventure in London… I wanted to let you know how I got my new position; it came about when I was talking to one of the junior guys that works in our call centre, he's a good kid, smart, but we couldn't offer him full time work, so I called the head of our biggest competitor company.

On my recommendation he offered him a job. I was really pleased for him and myself for helping him out and thought nothing more of it. A couple of days later the head of our competitor phoned me back and asked me what MY plans were and if I wanted to go and have dinner. He offered me a job on the spot.

What pleases me most I guess is that it all came about from me wanting to help someone else, and that's come from following your advice… so thanks for that and for all of your great advice."

The guy who wrote me that email was just like you Google. He became the source, he helped someone, he didn't think of how it would benefit him, and his "value" in the universe increased as a result.

Your value is over $200 billion, Google. More people should be like you. I should be like you.

———ຫ———

Dear Google,

One more story. I was playing poker in Atlantic City once with a guy named Joe. He was a great player but he did one thing at the table, which was interesting. Another guy needed to exchange cash for chips. Joe sold him some of his chips, which is actually not legal to do at an Atlantic City casino.

Later I asked Joe why he did that. Joe said, "Always be the bank. Then people don't want to bet against you."

Joe was like you, Google. And his value increased because he was like you.

———ຫ———

Dear Google, one time I had a wet dream about you. I was trying to get a business I started acquired by you. I met with you and everyone in the meeting seemed so smart and the meeting was fun. We were all just riffing ideas. All in your name Google.

The meeting was in New York but some people attended via videoconference from San Francisco. It was like we were all in the same room because of some sort of teleportation power.

Later, when I was given a tour, I saw chefs working in a Kitchen. I saw people skateboard. I saw people with three or four monitors programming. Everyone was smiling. I even signed a piece of paper saying I would never write about what I saw. And then a week later it turned out I signed the wrong paper so one of your priests asked me to come back and sign another paper and I did because I don't want to have the wrath of God on me. Anyway, I'm writing about you now but I don't think you really care enough to sue me.

I woke up that night thinking I was in love with you. And I am. I even sent you an email at three in the morning that night saying I would do anything to be acquired by you. You didn't acquire me. Someone else did. I had to "settle". But I'll always love you, Google.

—\\—

Dear Google,

I don't know. I have nothing new to say to you today. But today I'm going to try to be like you all day. Thank you.

LIVE YOUR LIFE AS IF EVERYONE ELSE WAS GOING TO DIE TODAY

You ever have that dream where your credit cards and passport got in the salad bowl and are getting salad dressing all over them and your wife is cheating on you and your boss is yelling at you?

Yeah? Me too. Last night.

I'm traveling on business today. Actually, I already traveled. Today I have business to do.

I have one rule: never travel on business. You never make a dime when you travel on business.

The last half of that rule will not be broken today. I will not make a dime. But sometimes it's good to just put a "face to the name". I put that in quotes. It's like I have this big list of names that need faces taped to them.

I'm going to tape some names today. I'm going to say that to a random guy in the hotel elevator later: "I'm going to tape some fucking names today!"

194

No I don't know.

Here I am. Helloooo Boston.

If today were my last day would I be in Boston?

No.

But why do people always say that? LIVE TODAY AS IF IT'S YOUR LAST! It's like a rallying cry for the world. Be happy…OR DIE! An anthem. Like the Partridge Family's "Take me Back to Albuquerque", or Queen's "We are the Champions". Those are anthems.

I picture the girl in Schindler's List yelling, "Goodbye Jews!" "It's Your LAST DAY, JEW!" "LIVE YOUR LIFE LIKE IT'S YOUR LAST DAY, JEW!"

If it were really my last day I would walk outdoors naked somewhere. For the fun of it I would tape two-dollar bills to my stomach.

It was 3am, after my salad bowl dream, when I was thinking of this. I told Dan the other day, "if you wake up at 3 in the morning thinking stressful thoughts tell yourself, "it's 3am and probably my thoughts are irrational so I'm going to make an appointment with myself to reconsider these thoughts again at 3pm" The idea is that at 3pm those thoughts will seem totally irrelevant."

Note to self: address salad bowl dream with credit cards sinking at 3pm. Further note: you might die today. Live it up! Goodbye Jew!

Claudia was sleeping next to me. I started to think if we got in a car crash what if I didn't die. What if SHE died? Now we are talking about something here. Because then I would be alive and I would have to deal with it. I would be sad and cry. I was thinking, "I hope I will be nice to her today just in case we get in a car crash later and she dies."

So that's my golden rule today. I'm going to live life as if everyone else is going to die. For everyone I meet today I'm going to really imagine that today is his or her last day.

THEN I WILL:

- Be kind to them
- Try to help them be less stressed
- Try to fulfill their dreams for the day
- Not talk badly about them. Don't talk badly about someone about to die. Too soon!
- Hug them if it's appropriate. Or kiss them. Not the people I'm going to "business" with later. That might be too much. But I will be nice to them anyway.
- Really listen to them. I will listen to everyone's last words today without interrupting them. Even if I can finish their sentence because I am light years ahead of them I will let them finish their sentences without my stupid voice piercing the air with its presumption.
- Learn from them. I will picture as if some universal life force is speaking to me through everyone else. I will listen carefully for clues that I can piece together later. These are the only clues that god will ever give me so don't interrupt.
- Don't opinionate all over them. What does it matter if I change their minds today? Do they really need my fantastic thoughts? They are going to die anyway

I feel like my life will be better if I practice living it as if everyone else is going to die today but I'm going to live forever. Floating in space eventually, with only your last words to cherish.

When you die, can I kiss your forehead? And when you finally close your eyes for the last time, my poor baby, I hope you can return that kiss to god when your eyes next blink open.

Make Every Moment a Work of Art

I am going to give you three techniques that if you use them you will be able to pick up any woman in the world within thirty minutes.

It doesn't matter if she is 90 years old or 21 years old. Ugly or beautiful. Married or lesbian. It doesn't matter if you are even a married lesbian. Don't view that as an obstacle.

I was sitting with Tim. We had just taken a ride in his new Lamborghini and I was about to throw up.

The speed limit was 15 because we were in a school area and it was lunchtime so kids could be randomly crawling on the street.. When we hit a speed bump he said, "I just did $2000 worth of damage to my shocks" and then he gunned it to 120 miles per hour while I tried to hold on.

A guy in a bandana wrapped around his face was unloading stuff from a truck and turned his head to watch us.

What if I were wearing a bandana to cover my face also and I just stared back at him the whole time? What if we stared at each other in slow motion?

What if we became friends after that? But never looked at each other's mouths because of the bandanas.

Tim and I went into his kitchen. Another guy showed up. New Guy. They started talking about a guy we all knew but I didn't know they knew him.

It's a tiny world. I can fit it in my pocket when I'm happy.

"That guy makes $30 million a year?"

"Yeah," New Guy said. "He tells people they can use his techniques to pick up any girl. He gives them a 50 page book for free and he says try it out. Then if you like it, you can sign up for a $5000 boot camp. My cousin did it. He rolls it in."

"Did it work?"

"I don't know. He says it did. But what if it's a placebo affect?"

I don't know.

You could give me all the placebos in the world and I never would've been able to pick you up, my beautiful little buttercup.

"What did they have him do?"

"They would take people to the Gansevoort Hotel, the upstairs lounge. Then they'd have to go up to girls and talk to them. Remove the barriers to confidence."

That's no problem, I thought. I have my own version of confidence bootcamp.

I did it myself a few months ago. I never advise people on something I don't try myself.

I dressed in a nice suit. I was a bit nervous. I went down to Wall Street.

I stood at the corner of Broad and Wall Street. I held out my hand and went up to people and said I was down on my luck and could I please borrow 5 dollars. "If you give me your card I promise I will mail you five dollars tomorrow."

Everyone's eyes would go crazy. The crazier their eyes, the

more confidence I was building.

Not a single person gave me money. For a while I lay down on the sidewalk and held my hand out and asked for money. People walked around me.

It was a bit embarrassing. One person I used to work with walked around me while I was on the ground. I said, "Oh, hey Dave. How are you doing?" But he just kept walking.

I don't know.

I was trying an experiment. A lot of people want to figure out an easier way to live. A way that doesn't conform. Where they can make their own rules. Not answer to a boss.

And have enough confidence to ask out the beautiful girl. Or guy. Or lesbian. Or whatever.

So I put it to the extreme. Go to the richest corner in the entire planet. Where ten trillion dollars in bailout money was airdropped right on that corner.

And ask for five dollars. Maybe get ahold of some of that trillion. The 15 minute work week.

Is it too much?

Finally, I was about to give up. I had no money.

I went up to a homeless guy straggling around.

Like, if he took a crack pipe and smoked and then you took the crack pipe you might have to use hand sanitizer. He had a garbage bag with his clothes in them.

I said, "excuse me sir, I'm having a bad day and I need five dollars. Do you have some money you could loan me?"

He reached into his pocket and started pulling out worn out one dollar bills. The sort of one-dollar bills that might've been made in a copy machine. He was going to give me money.

I felt bad. I said, "no, that's ok. Don't worry about it. " And he went off.

That was the only person who almost gave me money.

For fun, some friends were videotaping the entire thing from a distance.

At one point a Wall Street trader threatened to sue me once he realized I had guys videotaping in the background. He was very upset people might think he wasn't going to give me five dollars.

I was feeling very shy beforehand. "Don't worry," Christina said. "Just start asking people."

This isn't a story about Tim's Lamborghini. He blogs about it enough and I'm proud of him.

Nor is this a story about how everyone on Wall Street wouldn't give me money. They are just trying to get by themselves. Everyone wants to grab a tiny bit of happiness without being bothered by me.

This is not even a story about getting confidence.

Although if you want confidence, nothing beats asking 300 people for five dollars in the middle of the day on the richest corner of the planet Earth.

This is a story about trying to make every day a work of art.

Turn a few hours each day into a memory instead of a cubicle. Something you can laugh about.

And then write about.

OBSESSION

I timed it so I would walk past Lisa's house precisely when I thought she was going to leave. She wasn't there. So I walked around the block. I passed her house again. Still no Lisa. Hmm. I walked around the block again. Maybe she was taking a long shower and forgot what time it was. It was time to go to school and run into me in the street so she would love me. Still no Lisa.

We were in a relationship. But it had only started about two weeks ago. A few days ago I was happy just holding her hands and lying in bed. She said, "lets go out and hang out with our friends. This is boring." She didn't think we were in a relationship. "Don't tell anyone about us," she said. It was our secret.

The next girl I dated had a crush on my PhD advisor. But he didn't like her. "You aren't tenure track enough," she told me. "I mean, look at you."

So that was a little secret also. Nobody could know. She was also going out with a guy who was married. "They have an open marriage. His wife is very sweet. We shop for clothes together," she said. "But don't tell anyone."

The next girl was from India. She had a heavy accent and acne all over her face. But to me she was an exotic princess. "If my parents find out I'm going out with a white boy they will murder me," she said. So I had to walk at least ten steps behind her when we were in public.

"Your parents are 20,000 miles away," I said, "how would anyone know about us?"

"All these Indians you see here are related. Its one huge gossip network. If even one Indian sees us then my parents will know."

She showed me how to cook Indian food once. "You make potatoes and spinach. And then there are these five spices my mother gave me. Put all spices on. That's Indian food."

The next girl, Amy, had two parents who were psychotherapists. That means four different people were constantly analyzing me. The parents. The daughter (who had absorbed 20 years of psychotherapy at the breakfast table) and the psychiatrist they all required I visit. Since her father thought I was crazy.

It was because of Amy that, indirectly, I never worked on the IBM computer, Watson, that just defeated Ken Jennings, the Jeopardy super-star, on the Jeopardy TV show a few weeks ago

At the time, 1991, IBM was working on the chess computer Deep Blue, the computer that would eventually beat Garry Kasparov, the world chess champion. The developer of Deep Blue was my former office-mate in graduate school, Feng Hsiuh. But we all called him "CB", for "Crazy Bird". I have no idea why.

Deep Blue was called "Chip Test" when we were office mates and it was already the best chess computer in the world even then (1989). I would play it all day long rather than go to classes.

When CB moved over to IBM I had an idea for Deep Blue. I said, "don't have the program analyze every move. Why don't you skip a move and see if in some of the resulting positions, you win. That implies the computer had a threat. You can then back up and first analyze all of the moves that are threats before you start analyzing other moves. This will make the software much faster. "

They liked it! I was offered a summer job for $3000 a month. Triple the amount I had ever made before. I was gong to be rich! What made it even more real was that I had to take a urine test. It was IBM. I was in the big leagues. I was important enough now that someone even wanted to analyze my urine. I told my parents about the urine test and they were very proud of me.

I turned it down. I wanted to be with Amy. Amy was very predictable. I knew exactly when she would be passing my house on the way to her Japanese classes. I would bump into her every day. By accident. We didn't last the summer. "You're not an outdoors sort of person," she told me, "and Lance is." Lance had a nickname. "Tri-pod." Because of a particular body part.

Lance.

If I had gone to IBM not only would I have programmed the best chess computer in the world but also I would undoubtedly have played chess every day. It would be the most amazing dream come true.

Then, when that project was over, I would've probably worked on more projects for them, ultimately leading to the most recent Watson project. I would've been IBM's gaming king. I'm sure of it! Then, who knows what games I could've created for IBM.

Ten years later I got an email from Lisa. The first girl mentioned above who wanted me as her special secret that nobody could know about. I hadn't heard from her in a decade. She was dying of cancer and she decided not to take treatment. She had moved back in with her parents in Toronto. She sent me a picture of herself with her boyfriend. She seemed really happy.

I never knew any young person who had died before. I wanted to respond to her but I didn't know what to say. Every day when I looked at my email I felt ashamed that I wasn't responding to her. I was dealing with my own issues at the time. A few months later I read on the World Wide Web that she died and that the university where she worked was setting up a memorial for her. Someone wrote, "Lisa was the sunshine of my day."

What if I had run into her back in the day, when I was circling the block fifteen times in a row. The cars going back and forth wanted me to run into her. They whispered to me, "She likes you. But it's a secret." That one day I would've made her laugh. She would've realized how foolish she was for avoiding me and not returning my calls. "It was all a test," she would tell me. "I just wanted to see if you really loved me."

Maybe that would've changed everything. She would still be alive, having beaten the cancer with my encouragement. And IBM would now have a world champion robot for "Dancing with the Stars" because of my amazing programming skills.

For the briefest of moments, anything could've happened. And all life would have been different.

STEVE WYNN AND THE LOST DIAMONDS OF AFRICA

You know the movie I'm talking about. It starts off in some African village. Always in Africa. Women are doing the laundry. Men are either sitting around or doing some hard work with a rusty wrench. Kids are playing around a hose that wiggles its way through the only dirt street like a snake. Maybe someone is picking something in a field. Then we hear a rumble. Everyone looks up. People start running but somehow they all end up in the middle of the street, exactly the point they were supposed to be running away from. Soldiers of some sort, ranging in age from 12 to 25, come up in jeeps, horses, maybe little tanks, they swarm through the village. It's a big surprise. Nobody expected the soldiers there. The soldiers themselves seem surprised at their luck.

Then the gun firing begins. The soldiers are brutally and randomly kiling women, children, old men, while laughing. Depending on the rating of the movie, some women are chased. There is screaming in the background. Dust everywhere. Blood everywhere. A little girl crying "Mommy" but nobody holding her or comforting her. Blood in her hair. A boy, hidden behind tall grass, watching everything while the idyllic life he had known until that very moment crumbles all around him.

I've seen this scene in at least five movies. Blood Diamond, for instance. And Lost (ok, tv show). Others. I've spent at least $200 on movies so I can see this scene. I've hired babysitters so I can go to movies, buy popcorn, and watch this scene.

It's the scariest thing we can imagine. That's why they keep making it over and over. It's foreign, it can't possibly happen to us. And yet. And yet, if not but for the grace of god... we think. We could have been born there. Or maybe it can happen to us. Or it did happen to us. We're all human. We can relate to the suffering.

And then we think: it did happen to us. At some point we looked around and what was once our life has now crumbled. It's fallen apart. The soldiers, so irrational, so young, so brutal, so uncaring, have destroyed everything in our lives. We fall for the scene because it has the double-truth: it will never happen to us. It's always happening to us. "But not that bad!" we think. We hold onto that truth but it also crumbles, along with the women and children. Our brain speaks in relativity. It translates the blood on the screen to the constant shattering of our dreams.

We eat the popcorn. We have to watch the next scene. Someone is brave. Someone comes through the other side. There's revenge. There's redemption. There's a search for identity:

Who are we when the clothing of our hope is ripped from us and we stand naked facing death? We need to find out. It's worth the $200 across five movies (ten?). When all hope is lost we need to learn who we are, how to begin anew, how to stitch together the fabric of dreams that have been torn apart.

Which reminds me of another scene in another part of the world. Nora Ephron wrote about it. She was touring Steve

Wynn's art collection in Las Vegas. Wynn is notorious for not only being perhaps the best art collector in the world, but blind. Or on the verge of going blind due to a degenerative disease that can't be cured. He shows the group a painting that he was going to sell to hedge fund art collector Steve Cohen for $125 million. Perhaps it's his blindness, perhaps clumsiness, perhaps it's a secret desire to sabotage himself, perhaps he's just wondering where his wife is – he backs up and sticks a pencil through the painting, creating a $125 million hole in the middle of one of Picasso's masterpieces.

He calls his wife to tell her the news. He calls Steve Cohen, who says the deal is off. He calls the insurance company. They will pay him $30 million for the tiny hole made by his pencil.

Years later, a friend of mine visited Wynn in his apartment in Las Vegas last week and saw the painting. "It's completely repaired," Wynn told my friend. A company went in and took every thread and one by one stitched it together. "It's as good as new," Wynn said. My friend looked at the painting and couldn't tell. "It did seem as good as new!," he told me.

But it isn't. We remember the hole. We know for a fact it's not the same as the last time Picasso blew his breath across the drying paint. There's a psychic hole in it that will never be repaired, no matter how many nano threads are cosmetically sutured so as to show no scars. "Ahh, who cares," Wynn told my friend, "I love this painting too much anyway to sell it." And he did, after all, get $30 million and still got to keep the painting.

At the end of the movie, the one with the African women and children, we get to keep the painting also. The boy that was hiding. He survived. He grew up. And through the arc of identity we assume so casually in movies but is so impenetrably difficult to accomplish in our own lives, he's now a man of accomplishment. He's found his redemption. He can live with his psychic holes because after all, "he loves this painting too much".

The one that every day we can toss colors at. We can slice and dice with cubist thoughts, looking at a problem from every perspective until some hidden meaning is unlocked. Or not. We eat our popcorn, feel bloated, leave the movie theater, and go home. At the end of every day it's time to go to sleep. I kiss the forehead of my feverish daughter in the middle of the night. Please wake up okay, I whisper, and I promise I will always take care of you.

140LOVE – THE ULTIMATE DATING SERVICE

It was post-Stockpickr, post-my marriage ending, post-me disappearing from thestreet.com and the financial times, post-my worst-selling book coming out ("The Forever Portfolio") (see the story of that one and how it relates to dating), post the 2008 financial crisis. Post me spending the night at a motel in the middle of nowhere at the insistence of the police. The world was post-apocalyptic and we were now living in the radioactive fallout. No job was safe. No relationship left untouched. I didn't know where I was living. I didn't know how long I would live. The sunlight scared me. The survivors tried to put the pieces together. Or so it seemed to me.

I moved into the Chelsea Hotel. I'd leave it rarely, except at night. There was this gourmet hot dog place down the street, now shut down by the Department of health. It was my lunch every day. The rest of the day I'd read or look out the window. When I was a kid I would spend time four blocks away from there at my grandparent's house. I asked my grandfather once where God was and he pointed out the window, "over there." I think now maybe he was pointing at the Chelsea Hotel, where I was living.

I was dating. And becoming an expert at it. I tried every

dating service. I went out with the former Serbian Olympic Swimming Champion. We met on J-Date. I went out with another woman who was a judge on some TV animal show. We met on J-Date. I tried e-Harmony but I was subhuman for the e-Harmony folks. I wanted harmony in my life.

On e-Harmony they make you feel out this questionnaire for what seems like five hours but in reality was probably more like four and a half. And then finally at the end they told me the bad news via a popup. "Our statistics show that people who list their status as 'separated' are unlikely to find a stable relationship using our service.' They DOOMED me. What a mistake that was. Why couldn't they tell me earlier? Then I would've lied. I was ready to get married again. I wanted to meet someone and get married.

I met one girl who fought terrorists for a living. I met one girl who had just divorced a $100 millionaire 20 years older. I met one girl who hadn't worked in 20 years but lived in a beautiful apartment on the Upper East Side her father paid for. Another girl worked at a major bank and was willing to write whatever check it took for me to get divorced. I met two girls who were identical twins. One or both were lesbians. I liked the lesbian but dated the one that might not have been but she couldn't handle kids. Plus a friend of mine had gone out with one or both of them and I didn't like that and he couldn't even remember. Everything was through dating services. The magic of the internet was amazing. This is why they created hypertext. So we could all finally meet each other.

I'd spend two hours a night instant messaging, preparing messages, and looking at pictures. I wanted to meet someone.

During the day what did I do? Nothing. I had a job still at thestreet.com but never showed up for it. Once a week I still had to do something on CNBC or maybe that was already over.

I forget. I sat on a red-ripped chair. I tried to spy through the windows on 22nd Street to see if I could see anyone having sex. I taught one woman how to play poker in the hallway until random drug addicts asked us to be quiet because it was too late. I listened to another woman cry about how I would never be able to provide her a yacht on the Mediterranean (I thought it sounded too boring and I would probably get burned).

So I decided to do something new. Something I was truly passionately interested in. Something where I could make a quick 10-20 million dollars because I figured it was that easy. I was only interested in dating. So I figured I'd make an online dating service. I had read about how plentyoffish.com was made by one guy in his living room and now he was making one million a month. That could be me. That would be me.

Howard Lindzon had showed me a little website, twitter.com, over two years earlier in early 2007. You have to try it, he said. "Every time I take a shit," he said, "I put the details, size, etc. on twitter. It's hilarious. I have about 2000 people following my every shit." I didn't really get it. A year later I still didn't get it. But two years later I was starting to get it. It was useless. But another way to keep in touch with many people whom I would like but who would probably never be my friends.

I called up my old buddies in India, the ones who did Stock-pickr.com. They, of course, were happy to screw up yet another project for me and charge me as much money as they possibly could while doing so. So I sent them the complete spec of what I wanted. Howard was on board. He had over 100,000 followers so I figured he could help me get distribution.

The idea was: you'd log in with your twitter account. You wouldn't have to answer any big profile questions. And then people can browse your pictures and twitter feeds and determine if they like you and then send you messages through the service.

Also, every day we'd use an algorithm to determine your ideal picks and we'd send you the twitter IDs of your "perfect matches".

We got some investors excited and got enough interest to raise up to $500,000 or more. One of the investors was the woman who had started the very first online dating service, back in 1995. So we felt like we had a good thing going on. Also other people were interested in getting advice on how to manage their own twitter strategies so we named the company "140 Labs" so it would be more than just dating. It would be… everything! Some ad agency even wanted my help with setting up the twitter strategy for GM's Volt launch. Why the GM Volt would need to have a twitter strategy was not my business to ask.

One time I was at a dinner. Everyone was saying what they were working on. I said, "I'm working on a dating site for twitter." I thought everyone would start cheering and clapping. "What a GREAT IDEA!" they would say. Maybe someone would even present me with a trophy. I'm a winner. Then, the guy next to me said, "Wait a sec. I'M ALSO working on a dating site for twitter." And everyone started to laugh. I turned red. It was as if they all said, "you guys suck." Or even worse, "James, you suck. Because this guy is going to be the winner." I tried to patch it up saying, "well, twitter is a big world." But there you go, two twitter dating sites at the same surprise birthday dinner for Tim Sykes.

Meanwhile, GM wanted me to go to Detroit to talk about Twitter. And Jeff Pulver wanted me to speak at a conference about love and twitter. I was starting to feel anxious. I didn't want to go to Detroit. I felt like I was in the ad agency business again and I gave that up 10 years earlier. And I didn't know anything about love. What would love having anything to do with twitter anyway? That's like panties with shit on it having something to do with nudity. I couldn't waste time going to Detroit and I felt like a fake speaking at a twitter conference about love. What did I know about love? I was in the middle of a divorce. A few months earlier I had to be escorted to a motel by police. That's what I knew about love.

We launched the site. By this time I had poured about $50,000 into it. Which meant I was being completely ripped off somehow. A site like this should cost no more than $4000. But I was off my game, off my practice. I had a lot of things on my mind. I probably had eight of the nine happening to me on a regular basis. I had no chance.

People started to sign up. But it wasn't fast enough. Howard tweeted it, I tweeted it. We got about 100 signups. Then about 10 more. Then maybe 8 more. What's going on? Why not faster? Why weren't the servers going down because they were loaded with so many signups? And then it hit me: twitter is not anonymous. Look at this screenshot of these initial signups. Most of these signups were just friends but the point is: you can see their names. Dating services are mostly anonymous. They are like onions. You unwrap one layer at a time. First the mystery, then the sweet taste, then the identities revealed. Until finally you start crying.

So that's ok. I could be a dating service and maybe sell it to another dating service while I raise the money and build other twitter ideas since I now had twitter skills. And I could also be an agency. And I can make twitter games. And I wanted to buy a site called tweetizen. And...And...And...I could do everything. I could be THAT twitter guy.

Some money got wired in from investors. On the day the next $500,000 was supposed to be wired in I woke up shaking. Physically shaking as if the bed was vibrating. I didn't want to do it and my body was telling me. I couldn't take the money.

I couldn't put that $500,000 in the bank. Not worth it to then devote years of my life to this idea. I felt like I was going to vomit.

The whole thing was just a bad idea. I wired back the money that had been sent in. I emailed everyone else: "don't wire." The whole thing is off. Some people wrote back. "Why?" they were all set. They really wanted to wire even though I was telling them no.

I never responded. Josh Stylman, a well-respected entrepreneur, even wrote to me, "after all of our meetings I at least expect you to answer me why you don't want the money." I never spoke to him again even though we have many mutual friends. I feel guilty about that. I'm afraid to run into him in the street. I just didn't have an answer. My body was just shaking too much.

I shut it all down. The site itself lasted until about a week ago when Amazon's cloud finally shut it down. I don't think anyone found their true love on there. But it had been hard work and I needed a rest after that. Sometimes your head hurts so bad from all the people you disappointed, all the money you spent, all the energy that you wasted on a project that slipped away. It reminded me of the first date I ever went on.

When I was at the ripe old age of 17. It was in some summer program at a college (that was my definition of "summer vacation" during college. I let her cheat on my tests in Economics 101. Everything seemed so new and exciting. We saw the movie "Cocoon". We sat and made fun of all the other first dates. We had ice cream afterwards. We walked. That movie was so sweet, Sophia Lee said to me. But without the use of computers I had no chance. Despite "Cocoon" being 'so sweet", Sophia Lee didn't fall in love with me. And to this day I'm really upset that Sophia Lee never even spoke to me again.

FREEDOM

The rubber sheets wrapped tight around my bed were soaked with pee every morning when I woke up. I was four years old. I wet the bed every day. And I remember it clearly, getting that first bed. My dad carrying it into my room, replacing whatever cage had previously held me. Now I was free! My own bed! Every morning, my flannel pajamas soaked all the way through with urine and I'd have to peel them off. But I was four years old, I was totally free and the world was mine.

But then school. Then keeping your head on the desk during the naptime. A rap of the ruler on the head if you moved. Punishment. You can't play on the playground! Unhappy grownups with their husbands cheating on them perversely lashing out on the least powerful beings in their universe. We would all wink at each other in code. Rap! The teachers too smart for us. Punishment for pretending to be free.

Freedom again. Seven years old. Getting home from school. Getting on the bike. Riding until the sun went down. Random women (mom? Babysitter? Grandma?) yelling "Jaaames!" in the distance while I pretended not to hear. The icy sun wasting its last washed out colors of the day on aluminum suburban houses, dark street lamps, the reflectors on my bike, the last moments of my freedom for the night.

High school. I was free of the beatings of junior high school. All the schools in the area blended together. The little kids from the Jewish neighborhood mixed in with our torturers. We were beaten solidly for two puberty testosterone-driven years by kids in plaid shirts, sparse moustaches, the smell of the greasy underneath of cars, hair slicked back and girls whispering about each other's aborted pregnancies. We were soaked through in hormones and turning into monsters that would've been considered unbelievable before the radioactive age. 13 years old and I would've gladly volunteered to get any one of those girls pregnant. I would've sold them drugs or hypnotized them or paid them every last dollar of my allowance to get them pregnant: tall, blonde, slutty….and a guy in a denim jacket, two feet taller than me would elbow me in my back until I was down on the ground, "don't fuckin' stare at my girlfriend." But in high school I was free to stare.

But 9 to 3 classes. Boring classes. Who cares about Chaucer? Shakespeare the worst. I wish the Bronte sisters had died in childbirth. The most boring writing. Math was ridiculous. All I ever needed ever after was how to multiple and divide two digit numbers in my head. Do you ever need the Pythagorean Theorem for anything. Or an integral. Do I need an integral to get a check in the mail? To convince someone to buy something from me. The periodic table? WHAT!? I had been tricked again. High school was the worst prison. I asked Nadine Davis out. "no way!" I asked Debbie Dreger out. "Not in a 100 years!" and in that moment there was possibility because 100 years didn't seem so long to me. A prison sentence that long was conceivable when I was that young.

College! Freedom! No parents. Nobody to tell me what to

THE CHOOSE YOURSELF STORIES | *Freedom*

do. No standards to live up to. I could be morally decrepit. I could cheat, drink, girls would finally touch me. I could cheat on the girls who would touch me. But still tests, grades, money, loans, debt. I cheated to graduate college. I stole ramen noodles to eat. I needed somewhere to live so stayed with a girlfriend who wanted to despise me. I didn't want to work a real job so begged to get into graduate school.

Later, jobs. I was rich on $40,000 a year salary in NYC. I was a lowly programmer at HBO's IT Department but my answering machine said, "This is James Altucher from HBO." Girls calling me would think I was a movie producer. I was "from HBO". But I was in my cubicle. And my boss had a boss who had a boss who had a boss who had a boss who had a boss who had a boss who had a boss who had a boss. And that top guy eventually got fired. By who? God? It was a prison all the way through. I was told "you can't do that!" when there was something I wanted to do that would improve the company. I did it anyway. "You can't do that!" when I wanted to start a company on the side. "You can't do that!" when I would walk into the office of the CEO with him not there (now he's the CEO of Time Warner) and all of his passwords for every account were in his desk drawer. "You can't do that!" when eventually I left, escaping for the last time the jail of corporate America.

Freedom! When I sold my first company and made money. A lot of money. So much money I could give $100 tips to cabdrivers because I had nothing less and they had no change. I'd fly helicopters to Atlantic City. I'd buy paintings from my favorite realists without even bothering to negotiate. I bought a 5000 square foot apartment that was a sailboat factory in the 1800s and I rebuilt the whole thing. I was Free. I couldn't ever be killed. I was a demi-god.

But what a horrible prison housing a horrible person. I was worse than the man in the iron mask.That same 5000 square apartment wrapped around me like a tight cocoon when I went broke, every thread sewn by the caterpillar prison guard another regret, anxiety, tension, stress. INTC had bad numbers. Time to flee? Can I get a loan? My 2 year old daughter the jail keeper on my life. I couldn't even kill myself without the threat of ruining hers. So close to the gun range yet so far. Every smile I ever did for two years was a fake. The clown mask painted onto me before the big finale.

Finally! Sold my place. Now I could be a trader. The markets were mine. What freedom! I could wake up, trade at 9:30am, out by 9:35am, the day was done! What a lot of horseshit everyone else had to put up with, working their plastic jobs at the cardboard box factory. Except for those days when the trade wasn't over by 9:35am, wasn't over by 4pm on a Friday night. Wasn't over until next week and was horribly down. I lived next to a church. I never prayed in my life but I'd go there when it was empty and get down on my knees and say, "please let this trade work out!" Jesus Christ, please let INTC buy ORCL in the middle of a trading halt. Not a great trading strategy.

Freedom from trading! Started a fund of hedge funds. Freedom from worrying about crooked hedge fund managers! I started Stockpickr.com. Freedom from Jim Cramer, thestreet.com, and the cubicle nation on Wall Street! I left and started doing my own investments. Freedom from NYC! I moved upstate. Freedom from marriage! I got divorced. Freedom from all the constraints of every publication on the planet! I started writing a blog. With its worries about traffic and where can I syndicate and what can I pitch and what can I write every day.

When I write a "top 10" list people say I have too many lists. If I write how I screwed Yasser Arafat out of $2 million people say "link bait". When I bashed heads with Nouriel people say it was a payback post (it was, and I'm ashamed of it. I demoted the post to the ancient history of 4 days before it was published).

What's freedom? A cave? Minimal food. The soft touch of love without jealousy or need. Creativity with no self-critique? Breathing as deeply as possible and holding that breath for as long as you want – freedom from the central nervous system that forces you to exhale. A body that sleeps as long as you want. Laughter when you need it, laughter when you create it. Laughter when you tease it out of the people around you. A mountain you can look at but never have to climb. A breeze infused with the smell of toasted starch that whispers directly into your stomach.

None of these freedoms ever existed. The planet itself is a jail. Your body cell block H, your brain the 6'10" cellmate who will rape you at night and leave you bloody on the ground for his friends. The electric wire always ready to shock you back into reality everytime you see freedom within touching distance. Just once, to touch it and taste it. To smell it. But the senses themselves bind you until your funeral.

A funeral where the most delicious sound I'll hear from my perch in the afterlife will be the weeping of my own two daughters. They never realized how much they would miss me. A life in front of them where they will never be able to talk to me or see me again or laugh at any of my antics. They can't stop their weeping and what a beautiful orchestral sound that would be.

I'm 43 years old. Thank god I'm still alive. And loving every second of it with more passion than I could ever have imagined.

I Want My Daughters to be Lesbians

The other day a little boy – 11 years old – grabbed the head of my 12 year old girl and forced her to kiss him. She didn't want it to happen. As innocuous as it sounds, it was the first time her space had been invaded by someone of the opposite sex and it resulted in something very embarrassing and uncomfortable happening to her.

And it was my fault.

I wanted to go to the 50th birthday party of a friend of mine. She didn't want to go. She already had had a great day with her friends and she was tired. I argued: now you have to do what I want to do.

There were kids at the party so I thought they could play. She was shooting pool with me and I was on the other side of the pool table when the little boy came over and did his thing.

I couldn't react fast enough. I didn't even know how to react. But then I jumped over there and told the little boy to never kiss girls who didn't want to be kissed and chased him away from Josie.

Josie wanted to leave the party right away. So we left. A few minutes later, in the car, she was crying and she didn't know why she was crying. After we got home and parked I went into the back seat with her. I sat there next to her for a long time. She didn't stop crying

Girls don't know what goes on in the minds of boys and then men. Because of my rule "never go to weddings" I also never have been to a bachelor party. A friend of mine who is a stockbroker recently went to a bachelor party. "We all got a suite of rooms in Vegas," he said. "And a couple of prostitutes came over and went room to room and yanked us off." Maybe these are just stockbroker bachelor parties. I don't know.

This is the world of guys. I'm telling mild stories. Guys who read this are thinking, "wow! He's not even getting to the real stuff."

I remember as a kid, three honor roll students at my lunch table discussing the pros and cons of the following question: "if a beautiful girl was sitting in a room alone, naked, would you rape her?" This is what little boys think about. Boys who grow into men.

Women have their problems too. No relationship is easy. But guys until a certain age are only after one thing. And for some guys, that age is 80 years old. They hide it well. And they get it wherever they can.

I love women. There's nothing I would rather see than to see each of my daughters eventually bring home more women to share their lives with. Maybe I'm totally wrong and naive but I feel like women are nice to each other. The more women the better.

A couple of days later Josie was still upset. Would the boy talk about her in school? Would it happen again? Could she have avoided it? What should she have done? We talked some more for a bit. Then we went outside to play. Outside by the river, we ran into one of her best friends. They played soccer back and forth for about an hour.

When they were done, both girls were smiling.

How I Met Claudia

I was on one of my first dates after I had separated from my wife and the girl asked straight out what my net worth was within five minutes of sitting down. I had met the girl in an elevator the night before. I was walking into a building to visit another woman. I noticed this girl and I prayed to God that she would enter the elevator with me. She did. She hit floor #9. I hit floor #10. God is good.

Somewhere around the fourth floor she turned to me and said, "please tell me 2009 is going to be better than 2008". She was about five feet tall and had thick blonde hair, light blue eyes. I told her it definitely was. 2008 was bad for everyone in every way. It couldn't get worse. It was horrible for me, I said. I had gotten separated. A month earlier I had been on the floor in a fetal position and then put ads on Craigslist pretending to be a psychic. In my "psychic" capacity I told the future to about 20 different people. And probably tried to hit on ten of them.

I got off the elevator on her floor instead of the tenth floor. We talked for ten minutes. My phone kept ringing. My friend on the tenth floor (a woman) wanted to know where I was since the doorman had announced my presence about fifteen minutes earlier. Somewhere Between the first and tenth floor I got lost in a maze it would take me two months to exit.

My new friend's father had died during the year. And her husband, twenty years older, had cheated on her and divorced her that year. She was crying. She asked where I lived. I said, "The Chelsea Hotel". She said, "I've never had sex in the Chelsea Hotel".

My phone kept ringing while we were talking. "Who is that?" she said. And I said it was a girl who lived on the tenth floor. So I had to go.

The next day I sent her flowers and a teddy bear. I called her and we agreed to go to dinner.

Right away she asked me my net worth, what the specific details of my divorce were going to be, why wasn't I working, what were my plans for the future, what political party I was a member of, everything. I told her what I had going on. She was skeptical. She said, "Those sorts of things never work out." She asked me a million questions. I was honest about everything. She said, "I didn't think you were a good looking guy last night." Welcome to New York dating post-marriage.

Her conclusion: "you're completely insane. I can't go out with you." We went out for two months but she broke up with me at least once a week. It was really painful. I didn't have enough self-confidence to stay broken up. She'd break up with me in the morning and then call me later and say, "lets go out for a drink" and I would drop all other plans to go out with her again. I was drinking non-stop.

During this time, thestreet.com wanted to "rework" my contract, which resulted in me getting fired two years after I sold Stockpickr to them. The Financial Times lost their advertiser for the page I was writing on so they effectively fired me. CNBC no longer needed a bullish guy when the stock market was going down every day so they stopped using me. I let one business fail and started another business that was doomed to fail. I invested in a few other businesses but I had no idea then what would happen to those.

And still I kept getting broken up with at least once a week if not more.

My kids would come over every other weekend but since this girl would break up with me every Friday I had no idea what she was doing on a Saturday night and I'd get anxious about it. I'd arrange for my kids to get their nails done or something and I'd try calling this girl but no pickup.

I stopped returning calls from co-investors and my business partner, Dan, had to explain I was sick or busy, or dealing with divorce, or whatever he did to explain to people. None of my friends wanted to meet this new girl because they were all 100% sure that it would not work out.

I started meeting other girls via dating services to fill in the gaps when the first girl would break up with me. One girl was the host of her own TV show on ABC. Her dog shit on my rug. She wanted me to only wear suits. She wanted my teeth whitened. She wanted my hair cropped close to head (ugh!) "I've written a book on dating," she said, "so you have to have a certain look or else I can't be seen with you." "You need to be groomed," she said. It didn't work out. Anyone who looks at me can see I can't be groomed even if I wanted to. And being groomed like a dog is hard work!

Another girl asked me, "how do you deal with all the girls who want you for your millions?" And I was like, "i'm not sure where you're getting your information from but it's not what you think." That didn't work out. She wrote me a letter at the end (two weeks later), "you have mental problems and should see someone about that." She was a psychiatrist so she was an expert. She had said to me a week earlier, "If you use Ikea to buy furniture for your new apartment I'm going to have to break up with you." She had to break up with me.

Another girl I introduced to some of my friends. People I had been friends with for about ten years. During the evening she got so drunk her breasts kept falling out of her dress and she wouldn't notice at all. She would keep talking with her breasts fully out of her dress and people at all the other tables looking at us. So I walked her home. On the way back to her place she kept laughing and saying, "your friends really hate you. They only like you because they don't know who you really are." I got her into her apartment, dropped her on her bed, and then left and I still think about what she said and wonder if she was right.

I moved into a two-bedroom apartment so my kids could visit me. The last time they had visited me in the Chelsea Hotel I saw a used condom on the staircase of the hotel. Not a good environment for kids. The new apartment, right on Wall Street, had a bed for me, two beds for the kids, a couch in the living room, a table but no chairs and no other furniture. The kids and I would keep our clothes on the floor. We'd eat on the floor. We played Monopoly all day long on the floor. By the time they left each weekend the floor was covered with food, games, books, videos, whatever. And a housecleaner would come on Monday and clean up.

Then I'd see my friend again on Mondays and she'd break up with me on Tuesday.

I was exhausted of being broken up with. I was broken. It was like I had returned from outer space after a 12 year visit around the planet Mars. But the planet had undergone a nuclear war and everyone was radioactive so I couldn't touch them. "Isn't there anyone out there who isn't radioactive?" I would ask out loud but I had nobody to talk to. My apartment was empty. My day was empty. I'd walk around doing nothing.

I finally decided to take it seriously. No more second dates if I knew there was no serious relationship. No more drinking. Back to the Daily Practice, for the first time in three years. I defined for myself very clearly what I wanted. I liked being married. I wanted to meet someone I would marry. I'm an ugly guy and had no prospects in life at that moment so not the easiest thing.

It was a fulltime job for me. I spent three or four hours a day writing girls on various dating services. I wanted to meet someone. Finally there was a girl who had an interesting picture who said she was from Buenos Aires. This was on J-Date, a dating site for Jewish people. She was clearly not Jewish. I wrote to her and said she seemed really different. Maybe we could meet for dinner?

She said, "no dinner. Just tea." I wanted to push for dinner. Maybe something could happen.

"No. Tea!"

She was from Buenos Aires. I wrote and said, "Oh, I've always wanted to go to Brazil."

She wrote back and said, "That's nice that you want to go to Brazil but Buenos Aires is in Argentina. They speak Portuguese in Brazil."

We met for tea early in the afternoon one day. She told me she was into yoga and that's what she mostly thought about. She told me all the benefits she felt yoga had. How it was a spiritual discipline as well a physical one. She told me she would take me to yoga and I laughed and said, "maybe next lifetime". I told her how when I was a kid I was obsessed with trying to have psychic powers to see naked girls. I told her I had two kids. I told her how depressed I had been in my worst moments years earlier. She told me her stories. We talked for a long time and

228

it was nice.

We took a walk and sat down on a park bench in Tompkins Square Park. We didn't say anything to each other. We had already run out of topics to talk about. There was nothing but silence until she had to go. But I felt calm. It had been a very long time since I had felt calm. We must have sat like that in silence for about fifteen minutes. It's hard to sit in silence with someone but it wasn't hard this time.

Eventually she got up to go. She had to catch a train. While she was walking to the train she told me she was selling her house. I asked her where she was going to move. She said, "maybe the East Village".

No you aren't, I thought to myself. You're going to move to the corner of Wall Street and Broad. Where I live.

In a month from today we'll have our first year wedding anniversary.

FALLING IN LOVE

In retrospect she was a high-end call girl/grad student. But who doesn't sell themselves at some level? In almost every conversation we sell a tiny piece of ourselves. In the bazaar of interaction, we just hope for a tiny sliver of pretty silk back.

It was my very first shoot for HBO for the 3am project in 1996. I was nervous. The world at 3 in the morning was like a kaleidoscope of fantasy. It was the exact opposite of the day, where everyone wears their uniforms, follows their scripts, whispers their lines out of fear and out of neglect for the care of their real souls. When the sky turns dark blue, then black, the costumes disappear. You sometimes see right through to the skeletons.

This girl was something else. She was like a bird that ran straight into an electric fire. Sparks were everywhere. The city exploded with the darkness.

It was three AM, the corner of Houston and Ludlow, and she was dancing with random people on the street. She'd see a guy, she'd say, "I want to dance with you," and of course they would. She was pretty, blond, blue-eyed, and her eyes opened wider than her whole head. And who wouldn't dance with an electric goddess? She was dancing up and down the sidewalk. I had never seen anyone like her.

"Why are you dancing?" I wanted to know. "I passed a test". She was studying for a PhD in French literature. A useless degree, a useless language, if anyone had nothing in life to be proud of it was her but here she was dancing at 3 in the morning.

She had to put down her name on the release form I was required to get everyone to sign who we photographed and videotaped. Just in case the crack legal team at HBO needed to discuss anything with her. I took her release form the next day out of the pile of 20 or so I had interviewed and called her number and asked her to dinner. Completely unethical.

She said, "let me call you back in five minutes. No wait! Hold on!", and I heard a click and then she came back on after a minute and she said, "Yes, I would love to." Almost old fashioned, as if I was asking to court her. We walked for five hours that night. I made her laugh.

Right away I was in love. I told her so. She told me so. Maybe after one day or two days. I can't be expected to wait to say these things! Sometimes you just KNOW. Right?

What is there to learn about another person? We're all made out of flesh. We all need money. We all need health and sex and we all have issues and baggage that we inherited from our parents, our friends, their parents, our siblings, and even our siblings' parents. If I took a knife and opened your skull maybe I'd know all about you also.

She pulled me out of a box somehow. She unwrapped me and I saw that I was a beautiful present for the briefest of moments back so long ago.

"My last boyfriend," she told me on the second date, "used to pay me for sex. It turned me on."

"That's nice," I said. But I wasn't going to pay her for anything. I had no money.

Another time she told me she had once had a nervous breakdown so she ran outside naked and ran into one of her neighbors and within five minutes she was having sex with him.

"That's nice," I said. Because why wouldn't I say that. What a lucky guy that was! The next day, by coincidence, we ran into that guy with his young, new wife, in the street but he shook my hand and wouldn't even look at her and then he seemed to just disappear before conversation could erupt.

Another time she wasn't home when we were supposed to meet at 8pm. I walked up and down her tiny street (Cornelia St in the Village) until midnight. For four hours I kept ringing her bell every ten minutes, thinking that maybe I missed her enter. Maybe she had fallen asleep. I kept ringing the bell. Her neighbors would stare at me while I sat on the stoop to her building. I went home. At 1 am she called me and said, "can I come over?" And of course I let her. Why not? I wanted to see her.

My sister majored in French literature. My brother in law was French. I introduced them all to each other. I told my sister I loved this girl. The girl told my sister she loved me! I was so happy. She just "KNEW" as well. It was about four days after I met her.

I was going to marry her, have children with her, and grow old with her. We'd bicker but never fight. Maybe when I was rich I'd pay her to have sex with me and we'd laugh about that. Whatever happened to that guy that she dated? Did he stop paying her? Where is he right now? Is he married and thinking about her?

We saw each other every night, although sometimes she was busy at the library until 2 in the morning and then she would come over. Sometimes even until 4 in the morning. She was the hardest working French Literature PhD student I ever knew.

After about a dozen days she woke me up in the middle of the night. She had bunk beds for some reasons and we were squeezed together on the top bunk. I was afraid to fall off. "Hey!" she said. "Hey!"

"What??"

"You were saying out loud some other girl's name!"

She was unhappy about this. I couldn't help it though. I was sleeping. She said, "If you can say someone else's name in your sleep then I can also. I'm going to start saying other guys names in my sleep, anything can happen in my sleep, maybe anything can happen at ANY time, and we'll just see how you feel about that."

After I left her house that day I never saw her again. Sometimes you just fall out of love.

I HOPE TO GOD I DON'T REPEAT THE PAST

My dad's first marriage fell apart with him going crazy on the floor of his shit Bronx apartment. His brain fell apart. He threw things, he screamed. I've never once seen my dad raise my voice. But crazy can hit the human body like a tornado. Just like me, my dad's first marriage didn't work out (although for very different reasons).

Just like me, my dad's first business didn't work out. He went public with the business (a software business). At the IPO time he was worth $5 million on paper. He never sold any stock and eventually the stock fell to zero.

Our neighbor, Sandy Blatt, came over to our house on the day of the IPO. He said to me, "you know why I'm buying this stock? Because of this man." And he pointed to my dad. The stock never once moved higher. Sandy never spoke to my dad again.

My dad rented out a floor of the Plaza hotel to throw a party. He had a white tuxedo. He had two bands playing. Gary Becker, his #2, came up to me and said, "your dad is a genius." Much later Gary cheated on his wife, got remarried to another employee of the company, and then when the stock fell to zero never moved out of his sofa again until he died from depression.

I was too shy to talk to anyone at the party. I wanted people to like me, to know that my dad was throwing this party, my dad was a genius! But I sat outside in the lobby of the Plaza.

My dad joined something called the "Governor's Club". He paid $1000 a month so he could have lunch with the governor once a month. He wanted me to go once with him. But I had a paper route that bordered Christine Cardinal's paper route and there was no way I was going to skip those eight seconds where Christine and I would meet in the middle and I would smile at her, trying to elicit a smile back, a small movement of her lips, maybe some tongue (haha), so the governor could wait. And so would Reagan ($2000 for that lunch).

Back to his first marriage and the day it fell apart. He started smashing things, he was crying, he threatened to kill himself. He worked at the post office, he worked as an ice cream man, he was a failed classical composer, and he was obsessed with chess. He had nothing going on and now this. Now his life was more than over. It was a big negative. I wasn't there. But many years later he refused to tell me how bad it was.

So he went crazy crazy. The kind of crazy where police are called.

So the police come. Big guy. Bronx guy. Tough guy. "Seymour?" the policeman said, my dad lying on the floor: small, Jewish, thick glasses, kinked-up hair, crying although I prefer the word "weeping" (something sadder. We cry for many things but we only weep when we've lost something once dear – a love, our sanity, our vision of the future we clung to). And, coincidence of coincidences in a city of six million people, the police guy was the exact bully from sixth grade who used to pick on my dad.

"Seymour is that you?" And just then my dad had everything in the world to be embarrassed about. I'm sure he looked out the window, the light coming in. Can't the light reverse direction? Carry you out, back into the sun. Save you from this wretched planet. The Bronx, with cheating wives, a dirty post office, a mafia ice cream route, decades of ghetto Jews, decades to come of burnt out ghetto everything else. Back to Ra, who the ancient Egyptians said was father of us all? My sister, two years old, me not born for another 10 years in another ghetto borough.

Thirty years later my dad's business fell apart. He would burst into tears walking around a supermarket. He'd go to my younger sister's parent teacher conference and she would tell me later how embarrassing it was because he would start crying right in front of her teachers. How horrible it is to go broke in front of your children.

I went to visit and we'd play chess and he'd just say, "What's wrong with me?" when his moves were weaker than normal (he was a strong master in his day) and those moves never got better. It kept going downhill until he would make left turns on eighth avenue (his parents lived on eighth avenue – for his entire life you can only make a right on eighth avenue but he would start to forget). "What's wrong with you!" my mom would say.

Sometimes I'd get the call from him. "I'm missing," he'd say. And I'd drive out to whatever mall he was at and he'd forget where his car was and what he had bought and where he was going and I would pick him up and take him to the hospital and the doctor would always make everyone feel better, "Don't worry," until of course, dad was dead and the doctor was right – no more worries.

When I was ten my dad had surgery on his eyes. He had to

sleep and not open his eyes at all or he could go blind. I was told not to wake him. But I was ten. And I was playing with a tennis ball outside and it hit his window. He woke up. "James!" my mom yelled from the front door. My friend said, "good luck" and jumped on his bike and rode home.

I went in. My dad's room was dark. I stood in the middle of the room. My mom limped over to me (she had polio as a girl). "Stand still," she said to me but it took her time to reach me. My dad, bandages over his eyes, the room completely pitch black except for the glimpse of sunlight trying to peek through. I could barely see my mom standing right in front of me. "Hit him," my dad said. So my mom did, across the face. More than once. But I deserved it. I was afraid he was going to go blind now because of me. I deserved it.

Years later, I went crazy. I was throwing things. Alcohol had been ingested. I was angry. What a horrible thing for children to see. The police were called. "What's going on here?" "Nothing". "Well, something is. Someone called us." And I put up no fuss. Neighbor's lights clicked on as I was led out to the back of the police car. No leg room. What do they care?

They took me to a small motel on the side of a random highway about ten miles away. "Don't leave this room all night," the police said, "or we'll write this up and it will go on your record." There it is, that "record" again. When can I play funky music on that record, white boy?

I was so tired anyway. The room was spinning from alcohol. I slept and for awhile it was like I was sleeping in the cyclone at the amusement park. And when I woke up I had no idea where I was. I walked outside. It was six in the morning. No cars were on the highway. Nuclear war had destroyed the entire world. And the radiation had finally mutated me beyond recognition.

HOW I DISAPPOINTED TUPAC'S MOM

I really disappointed Tupac's mom. Although, to be honest, it was her manager. She wanted to do an enhanced CD of Tupac's unreleased songs. I don't know what it was with Tupac. People kept shooting at him. First, one of his testicles got shot off. Then someone finally got to him and killed him.

Rappers don't really shoot at each other anymore. Back then there was some idea that people who sang songs and played music were at war with each other. East versus West.

It was a marketing gimmick. If you were on the side of the "East" you bought songs made by musicians from the east coast. If you were from the West, you bought music made by people from Death Row Records. It was all marketing. And the marketing got even better when a few people got killed.

I once had one of these rap groups, Mobb Deep, come into my office. Their pockets had big bulges, like they were carrying fifty loaded guns in each pocket. Everyone had guns because that's what the marketing people at the record labels told them to do. Shoot to kill, they were told.

238

So now all that Tupac's mom had of her dead child that traveled through time and space to come through her womb was his unreleased songs. So she called her manager, who called this guy, Steve, who called me, to help them make an Enhanced CD of Tupac's songs. An Enhanced CD had not only songs but you could put it in your computer and do computer stuff – like watch videos, look at photos, and read things.

We had done some enhanced CDs. Big Pun, Wu Tang, whatever. I had the demo CD of everything we had done and I went to the manager's office. Steve was supposed to meet me there but he never showed up.

Here's the problem. I didn't know how to use a computer. I should be more specific: I had never before in my life used a Windows-based PC. I had only used Apple products and Unix-based computers. I majored in computer science, went to grad school for computer science, had worked as a programmer for ten years, ran a computer software company, but I had never used the most popular brand of computers on the planet

"Can you show me a demo?" Tupac's mom's manager asked me. I was jealous of him. He had it made. They were going to release this album and it would probably be the last album ever to sell ten million copies. What would he make? $1 per copy? And then maybe they would find more unreleased songs and release those.

"Can you show me a demo?" he asked again. I had the demo on me. I pulled it out of my plastic bag. But I didn't know what to do. I didn't even know how to open the slot in the computer that you put a CD in. And once I did that, then what? How would I find the demo CD on the computer. Do these things work like Apples? Did double-clicking on something work? Was I going to figure all of this out from scratch right in this guy's office?

I don't know how to use your computer, I said.

He looked at me. You don't know how to use a computer?

Well, I said, I don't know how to use your computer. I never used a Windows machine before.

You have got to be kidding me?

No, we have to wait for Steve. I'll try calling him.

This is a waste of my time. Why would we let you make Tupac's Enhanced CD if you don't even know how to use a computer? This is a joke.

So I put my demo CD back into my plastic bag and I left.

I went back to the office.

Everyone crowded around. They wanted to do the Enhanced CD for Tupac's unreleased songs.

"How'd the meeting go?" someone said.

I put my head down on the keyboard. Tomorrow I'd have to figure out some other customers to pitch. Maybe Con Edison would finally say yes. I hated rappers. They're always shooting people anyway. I wanted to do Con Edison. Tupac was going to be a $150,000 job. It was supposedly a done deal until it turned out I didn't even know anything about computers. At that point in our company's history that would've paid for about 1.5 months of payroll.

Or, if no customer could be found, maybe everyone would have to be fired and I'd have to go and beg for my old job back. But that would be failure. People would laugh at me behind my back. I took a deep breath and picked my head up.

"The meeting went well," I said. "Maybe it will take one more meeting to clinch the deal."

I Am The Bravest
Man Alive

Yesterday, 10pm, I was asleep and the opening of my bedroom door woke me up – my 9-year-old daughter was in a panic. "Something's wrong with Josie!" Josie is her older sister. Like any concerned father I tried to keep my eyes shut, "What?" I murmured.

"You have to come down!" she said.

So I said, "ok, ok, go downstairs. I'll meet you there."

She closed the door and went downstairs.

Five minutes later: "Daddy! You have to come down!"

So, ok, I woke up, put my pants on (when I'm home I wear the same pants every day until they are so frayed that no Laundromat will even touch them). I went downstairs. In Josie's room, she's lying around reading a book.

"What seems to be the problem here?"

Both kids pointed at her wall. There was an insect, frozen in fear at these two enormous giants that had been yelling at them. The insect was about twice as big as an ant but maybe smaller than a bee.

"Look!" they yelled.

In 2008, Josie once sent her then 6-year-old sister into the kitchen. Her mother and I had been screaming at each other. Actually, I was probably the one doing the screaming. My throat, lungs, heart were raw. Everything was raw to the bone and within days we'd be separated forever.

"Daddy," Mollie said back then in 2008. She was so tiny, a little girl with nothing but orange hair surrounding all over her. Sort of like "The Thing" in the Addams Family TV show when I was a kid. "Daddy, Josie wants to know if you two are getting a divorce." Her sister had sent her in. Josie was nowhere to be found. They were so scared of the yelling, the fighting, the uncertainty of what would happen to them. What would happen to us, to me, to their lives, so little and unprotected by the two adults yelling. I didn't know what to say to her. She was trying to smile but all there was fear.

And now again, Mollie on her mission for her sister who was three years older than her.

The insect.

"Ok, ok," I said, and then I started yelling, "I see the seriousness of this situation here. There's a living being one- ten thousandth the size of you guys and it happens to be motionless on the wall. I think I might be the only one on the planet brave enough to handle this situation."

Their room was a mess. Comics, clothes, books, pens, crayons, shit all over the place. I walk into their bathroom, which posed a much greater threat since someone or both of them had just used it and everything in their bodies must've have exploded out. It was as if they had eaten diseased moose for dinner and diarrheaed it all out. Then they decided that Mollie, the younger one, would immediately get me to kill an already dead insect that was on the wall next to Josie's bed.

I got the Black Raid. I sprayed the insect. It fell to the floor.

"It's still moving!" Mollie said. I got toilet paper and picked up the insect and flushed it down the toilet.

Josie finally spoke, "now that side of my bed smells like insect repellant."

"Listen," I said, "what you just observed was probably the bravest act in mankind that you two children will ever observe. I just destroyed a monster that was maybe threatening not only your sanity but your lives."

"Daddy," Mollie said, "aren't you supposed to be asleep now anyway. Why are you talking so much?" My use was done.

"I can't believe the act of bravery you two just observed," I said. And then using the Black Raid container as a fake microphone I began to sing into it, performing various ballads from different Broadway shows. This would be a warning to them in the future. Don't wake Daddy up!

When my musical repertoire was exhausted, I went back upstairs. It was pitch black in the room. Claudia was only half asleep – not moving but woken up by all the noise. She slurred in an accent I still can't place after knowing her for two years, "what's going on down there?"

"I just killed a furry, repulsive monster approximately 7000 times smaller than me."

"Mmm," she said, "that's nice honey." And she fell asleep.

She was in the middle of the bed. Men don't get the middle of the bed. One of these days I will find out what the middle of the bed feels like. I'm sure it would feel like there was balance in my life, that I was warm and protected and that every side of me was forming itself into a shape that would comfort me and hold me. But Claudia always ended up in the middle.

I couldn't sleep. I had just killed that furry little monster. It was dead now. And within 100 years, more or less, the 4 human monsters in this house will almost certainly be dead as well.

I'm Ashamed

I was very ashamed. Alex brought it up delicately. We were on plane coming back from some BS meeting somewhere where we were supposedly analyzing a company for our VC fund.

"I saw you put your apartment up for sale?" he said. He must've been looking at listings because he was in the market to buy. Only ten months earlier I had had a huge party at my apartment celebrating moving into it. Over 200 people were there. It was catered. We had a gym. Little kids were hitting the punching bag. My 2 year old was painting on her easel. People were shooting pool on the 1946 vintage pool table.

"What!?" I said, "that's ridiculous. We were just having a conversation with real estate brokers. We didn't tell them to actually sign us up." I acted infuriated.

That was a lie. Of course we had to sign paperwork telling the real estate agents to list our house, set a price for it, get an MLS number, take photographs, exclusively work with us, etc.

"Ok," Alex said and he sort of smiled because he knew I was

lying and I knew I was lying.

I went to look out the window of the plane. My face was burning red. Everyone knew I was a liar. Everyone knew I was a failure. The plane was riding just above the surface of the clouds, benevolent balls of cotton in the sky that seemed to be just barely holding us up.

I Had To Lie

We were 70 miles north, trying to find a place that was going to be in our price range. We were looking at places 1/3 the size of our old apartment (which one year after we had put it up for sale, still hadn't sold). Every house seemed worse than the next. I hated the real estate agent. After one place I got a call from one of the investors in our VC fund. He's now the CEO of Investcorp.

He asked me, "why aren't you putting money in the latest deal with the fund? We expect the partners to put money in each deal."

I was ashamed to say that I couldn't afford to. I had already lost enough money on that company. Another batch of money from me wouldn't save it or kill it either way. But would kill me.

I said, "my wife is making all the personal investment decisions. We've already put money in that company three times so she said, 'enough is enough' and you know, 'happy wife equals happy life' ".

Savio didn't buy it. He said, "come into the office next week. We need to talk"

Later we were all sitting in a café in the town 70 miles north. The real estate agent was talking about how great the area was. How great the schools were. I was depressed. If I didn't sell my house in the next three months I'd be at zero. It turned out to take about 4 months to sell from that point.

There was a girl in the café sitting reading a book. She was beautiful. I thought if I ever got divorced I could maybe meet her. We could read books. But at some point she would probably find out what a failure I was. How worthless I was to everyone around me. The real estate agent broke through my thinking, "the house even has a sump-pump. In case there is flooding."

—⧟—

When I finally moved upstate it took two years until I stopped saying, "I live in NYC." Then I would start saying, "I just moved up from NYC." Even though it had been two years. The train to the city was 81 minutes. The windows looking from the train out onto the Hudson River would change like a slot machine while I stared, hoping I would get lucky just once.

I met with one investor to see if he could put money into a new fund I was raising. Then we took a cab across town together.

"Aren't you all hooked up," he asked. "Can't you call one of your Internet friends with $100 million to put money into this?"

I didn't have an answer. He disappeared out of the cab when we got to his stop. It was raining. Gray. Dark. I was by myself in the back of the taxi. The driver was mumbling in another language into his phone.

Finally I answered, "I don't have any friends."

—⧟—

Years later, I lied again. I was meeting with Roger about some investments we were making together. He asked out of the blue, "So what's going on? Everything good?" And I said, "yeah". And he said, "Family good. Wife good?" And I said, "no issues".

He knew I was going through a divorce but I didn't want to say it and he didn't want to say it. I felt shame about it. This was a moment when I was failing at about five things simultaneously and didn't want to admit to any of them.

I went back to the Chelsea Hotel where I was staying. At around 1am the phone rang and woke me up. I didn't pick it up. The girl I was dating said, "who is calling at one in the morning?" And I was afraid that I couldn't answer. I had no idea. It could've been trouble to pick up. The phone rang nine times and stopped. She was upset, "who is calling??" It was my birthday in 2009. I was too nervous to have a coherent answer so she packed up and left.

When she was gone I called downstairs and asked who called me. It turned out out to just be Timor from downstairs. He said, "you have to move tomorrow to another room. It's day 30 and it's a NYC law."

"I thought you always break that law. That's how we used to do it."

"Yeah, not anymore."

So the day after, I moved. My new "apartment" in the hotel didn't have a door on the bathroom. But at night I could turn the lights out and see into the backs of the apartments on 22nd Street. A few times I thought I saw people that were naked but I was never sure. Just bodies moving around. Continuing their lives and routines while I sat in the dark and watched.

—m—

I got tired of being ashamed of things. I give up. I don't want to be ashamed of anything anymore. Shame is not who I am. It's just an ugly sweater I wear. Time to change sweaters. When I wear the same clothes too many days in a row, Claudia reminds me to change clothes. "You smell too much."

Shame is one of those things that are hard to change out of. We cling to it because it feeds something inside of us that we are afraid to give up. It feeds our perfectionism. It feeds out hypnotized visions of what success is. It's a Halloween costume that we think looks better than our real self. But it doesn't. It's cheap plastic nylon whatever. Shame, and pretending to be perfect, limits our freedom but nobody taught us that in college.

And it oozes from the pores in our skin and the smell is unmistakable. Time to shower. Time to breathe in other smells. Time to be naked.

THREE STORIES ABOUT BILLIONAIRES

A) Jealousy. I was out for breakfast with a friend of mine who manages some money. About three billion dollars. He's done very well and written a book about his success. Nice guy.

At the breakfast he told me that the day before he had had breakfast with XY [Insert top billionaire's name who runs a multi-billion dollar private equity fund]. My friend was describing that breakfast to me, "the entire time he was going on and on about what bastards 'those Google guys' are. As in 'why should those google kids be worth $18 billion each and I'm only worth $2 billion?'

People think a billion dollars will solve their money-envy issues. But having a billion dollars could actually make it WORSE. You never develop the muscle for "I-will-never-have-a-billion dollars".

When you have a well developed "i-will-never-have-a-billion-dollars" muscle you maybe find other things in life aside from money that will fulfill you – having positive people in your life that you love, being healthy, being kind, not taking things so seriously, giving up control over things you can't control, and so on.

B) Enough. Joseph Heller, the author of Catch-22, once was at a party in the Hamptons. A guy came over to him and pointed at a young, 25 year old standing in the party who worked for a big hedge fund. Heller's "friend" said to him, "see that guy over there? He made more money last year then you will ever make with all of your books combined."

Joseph Heller said, "Maybe so. But I have one thing that man will never have."

His friend was skeptical. "Oh yeah, what?

Heller said, "Enough."

I think this is beautiful. What is enough? It's not a number. Look around you this second. Do you really need anything else then the feeling you have this second? If you say "money" or even "sex" or "love" those answers might be true for future seconds. But right this very moment do you really need more money in your pocket? You might be on a train reading this book. How would you be having sex anyway? Often we get absorbed in the things we want in the future. As if we are unhappy now but there's some complicated journey that can take us to happiness. The currency of unhappiness will never buy us happiness.

Often to get to happiness, we can skip the journey part and just choose to enjoy this moment. This moment we can have "enough". Why not? Who can stop us?

C) **Blood.** A friend of mine was a professional dominatrix. I have more about her and how I met her in an upcoming post (she was girlfriends with my neighbor at the Chelsea Hotel).

She and her girlfriend once gave me a tour of the dungeon that she worked at. In one room was a coffin. She said, "we have one client here that likes to get in the coffin and then get it filled up with cement while he is in there and he's wearing a mask he can barely breathe out of." Ok, to each his own. That's not what this story is about.

But if you are a professional dominatrix and you meet me, trust that I am going to ask you to tell me a story. Here's one story she told me, "I had a regular client who was a famous movie director. Everyone in the world knows his name."

"He has a huge Park Avenue apartment he stays at when he's not in LA. HUGE. I got there with all my equipment, including a knife. All he wants is for me to cut him all over his body until he is bleeding. By the time I was finished, his entire foyer was covered in blood. I was even worried he might die. But, of course, he didn't. I just saw his latest movie."

One thing that this shows me is that a billion dollars doesn't mean you can buy an expensive apartment. You don't need a billion for that. And you don't' even need an expensive apartment. But what a billion dollars does do is allow all of your qualities to be magnified. Bad qualities and hopefully good qualities.

I don't judge this guy for wanting to be cut. Or the other billionaire for being jealous of Larry Page. Heck, I'm jealous of Larry Page.

But its just clear that not having a lot of money is just an excuse people give when they feel frustrated, or not at the right place they feel they should be in their lives, or stuck somehow ("if only I had a lot of money, I could do this great idea I have"). Giving someone a lot of money will only remove that one excuse they had. Then they will find other excuses for the reasons they are unhappy. (e.g. "I need to almost bleed to death to be happy").

Veronika tried to explain this guy's motives to me. "He has to make decisions all day long. That's all he does is make decisions and have total control over the people in his life. For the short while he is with me, he gets to lose his sense of total control. I take control."

My guess is there are other ways to give up the feeling that you need to control everything in your life. We want to control but we can't. Most of the time we resist the thing that life throws our way.

"Why is this happening to me?" is a common question asked since the dawn of time and there is only one answer: "Because!"

If you can find, this second, ten things to be happy for or to be grateful for then you will finally achieve what 99% of the population never achieves, at least for this single moment: Enough.

WHY A GRENADE NEEDS TO GET THROWN AT ME

I was at another dinner and the guy who bought and runs a major chain of yogurt stores in the United States stared straight at me, past about five other people in between us and said, his face slightly red, his voice raised, "I've done two tours in Vietnam. Nobody should be pontificating about wars if he hasn't had a grenade thrown at him."

I really do not want a grenade thrown at me so maybe he's right. I don't want a grenade thrown at my kids ever either. And if that means they can never talk about war, then I guess that's one of the things they will have to give up in life, along with heroin via needles, masturbation via asphyxiation and ever getting into a car when a teenage boy is driving. I have made it very clear that these things are off limits.

Some conclusions: I probably should avoid dinners. I get into a lot of trouble at them. Was it really so bad to say the simple sentence: "I can never imagine a situation justifying sending my 18 year old child to a place where a grenade is going to get thrown at her."?

256

And then I wondered about other things I said at that dinner and now I feel even worse. I said that maybe Israel should've been put in Montana. The US could've handled it. And then we wouldn't have all this bloodshed in the Middle East. And the Israelis would have a much bigger plot of land to do their thing on and not have to worry about constantly being attacked. Is it any wonder that Jewish people in the US are much more involved in culture and the arts and innovation than Jews in Israel? It's because they always have to worry about being bombed there! Would Wyoming bomb Montana? Maybe, but I doubt it. Is Wyoming even next to Montana?

But now I realize that the host of the dinner, who I have much respect for, is part Israeli. In fact, to top off my humiliation, I think her mom was "Miss Israeli". Did I offend?

I really need to stay home at night. I don't even drink. And yet these things come out of my mouth. Like that movie with William Shatner where everyone had tarantulas coming out of their mouths in this small town and he had to use all his Star Trek and Twilight Zone martial arts skills to save the town.

The guy sitting next to me was a co-founder of foursquare. I asked him if he regretted not taking $100 million off the table when Yahoo offered it about a year ago. He said, "things are going great at foursquare." That's a great non-answer.

Another guy walked in. This was at the cocktails pre-dinner. I asked him what he did. He said he was a businessman. I said, "That's funny. You look like a politician. As soon as you walked in I said to myself, 'that guy is in politics'." He was tall, gray hair, blue suit, red tie, thin.

He said, "Well … I just finished a stint as Governor of Kansas."

Another guy said, "How did you know he was in politics?"

And I said, "look at him. He looks like the opposite of me

and NOBODY would ever say I was in politics."

And then I wondered, "That must be fun to have a "stint" as a governor." Sort of like a tour of duty in Vietnam with no grenades.

I asked him, "was that fun being governor?" And then I felt bad because that's the sort of question I would ask governors when I interviewed them when I was twelve years old. In the 31 years since then my interview style hasn't changed at all.

"Yes," he said, "I loved the policy side of it. But I'm a businessman at heart." Good guy. Something about Kansas makes people good guys. Maybe Israel would've done ok staking out a part of Kansas. Everyone would've left them alone I bet. The ex governor of Kansas made some anecdotes implying that the cost of living in Kansas is about 1/6 that of the cost of living in places like DC and NYC. I might want to move there. I wonder if they need a chain of yogurt shops there.

I was a bit harried when I got to the dinner. I had just been on CNBC's show "Fast Money". Some gloomy, suicidal guy, Dick Bove, said that "the end of times were near" if we don't come to an agreement about the "debt ceiling".

I said on TV, "no matter what they do over the weekend with the debt ceiling I'm still going to buy my kids candy on Monday and when the ipad 10 comes out I'm probably going to buy it." And then on twitter someone said if "someone got that guy hair gel he might actually sound smart" which I thought was an odd comment but unless someone has ever thrown a grenade at him I guess he's allowed to say it. Or not say it. I forget the subtleties of these things when it comes to grenades.

Dan, my business partner, and his dad were watching the segment. Dan told me later he turned to his dad right then and said, "James couldn't tell you three things about the debt ceiling and now he's on national TV talking about it."

When I got home around midnight my kids were still up. I don't think they ever sleep. What do they even do? They don't have to work. Or plan things. Or even think about debt ceilings. Why are they always up puttering around? If I were a kid right now I would not waste precious time puttering around. I would sleep as much as possible.

We were going to a water park the next day. I tried on a bathing suit I had just bought. They were laughing hysterically when they saw me in it. I haven't worn a bathing suit in about fifteen years. Or shorts. I hate shorts. I grumbled something and went to sleep in my bathing suit upstairs. I had to break it in like a baseball glove.

The next morning, Claudia asked me how the show, the dinner, and everything went the night before. We were drinking our first cups of coffee. Outside it was gray, little specks of rain hitting the windows, the neighborhood cat peeking in the window on occasion. I said to her, one of these days I'm going to write a post and say it was quite possibly the best night this universe has ever experienced. And she laughed because that could only mean that many things had gone horribly wrong

THE YEAR I DID NOTHING BUT PLAY POKER

After I threw all her clothes down the garbage incinerator I went off to play poker at the Mayfair Club across the street. It was an accident. They were supposed to go to the laundry guy downstairs. But they were in a garbage bag. So you make the decision.

Then I went to play poker, which is what I did every day from the day after I sold my first company until exactly one year later. 365 days in a row without a stop, including the day my first kid was born.

I went down to the Mayfair club for the first time in September, 1998, and they didn't want to let me in. "Who sent you?" they said through three layers of antiquated doors and alarm systems. I didn't have anyone who sent me. I had nobody. For three years all I had done was work. I didn't have any friends at all. I sold my first company in August, 1998. I had no friends who could possibly send me anywhere.

There was no internet poker then. No poker TV. Just a bunch of old guys, some young ones, and some waitresses. I'd leave work at 5pm. Drop off quickly at my apartment which was two blocks away from my work on 20th St. (I like to set up my life so I have every convenience possible) and then I would say, "I have to go!". I ate out on 25th Street at that Indian place, and then I hopped on over across the street to the Mayfair which opened at 8pm. Around 2am we'd all order food from Sarge's, which was open all night. And finally around 4am everyone would stumble out.

If I felt like it, I could then go over to the Diamond Club then which had a similar alarm system and sat over on 21st Street. It seemed like they were open 24 hours a day to pick up whatever straggler still wanted to play a game. At least, I never saw a time when they weren't open. Despite the alarm system the Diamond Club had been robbed repeatedly, with people left on the floor in the underwear. I didn't want that to happen to me.

During the day I read every book I could find on poker. There wasn't much then. I also ordered videos. VHS tapes of every world series. "At least he isn't out with hookers," she would tell her mother.

The money was nothing. I didn't need it or want it. I started off playing $10-20 holdem. And gradually rose to $75-150 at the Mayfair. It didn't mean anything to me. I had just sold the company and money was burning thru me at a rate incalculable to anything my parents, girlfriends, or wives had ever taught me. Before it was all over, years later, I would be dead broke and calling my parents on the phone for a loan they wouldn't give me.

Over the summer we got a house in Brigantine. I would go down there on Friday, have dinner and then go to the Taj for 36 straight hours before flying home. On the helicopter ride over the pilot would circle the house we were staying at right on the beach and my 5 month old daughter would try to wave from the ground up to me although she would have no idea then or now what she was waving at.

At the Taj I would play $300-$600 one-on-one against a Vietnamese guy whose wife was constantly sitting next to him begging him to stop. She was nine months pregnant but I never saw anyone more beautiful. My biggest winning day and my biggest losing days were against him. We would go all night insulting each other and winning and losing pots up to $10,000. Every minute another pot. Someone told me recently he's in jail now.

Other times I would fly to Las Vegas with all of my new friends. The Super Bowl would be on ten screens all around, we'd be playing poker, and all drinks were free. Sometimes the authors of the poker books I was reading would be at the same table. Maybe for the first time I felt like what men feel like. Cards, sports, women, drinking. This was it, right? I was a man? It was my birthday that Super Bowl day.

When she found out I threw all her Easter clothes down the garbage chute she was upset at me. "I have no clothes for Easter now!" The baby was sitting in the middle of the floor crying. "I have to go," I said. Like I said on every such occasion. And I went down to the Mayfair while she was crying. At the Mayfair there was a rule, if a woman called asking for you, Ingrid at the front would say, "I'm not allowed to say if he's here or not."

Every night people would joke around the table. Nobody knew anything about anyone and we would all gossip when people weren't around. What'd he do to make that money? Or, this one was a criminal for years, went to jail, and now he's clean. People would look forward to seeing me. After awhile, I had the banter down. I felt like when they weren't taking my money they were my friends. Whenever I saw anyone of them outside of the poker room they all looked strange to me. They didn't look like real humans when under the scrutiny of broad daylight.

I stopped playing poker cold when I had another idea for a business. That business didn't quite work out. Everything happening to me then wasn't working out. I lost my business, I had no friends, lost my house, lost my money, lost my family, lost all of my pride. Right when I thought I was a winner, I was a massive loser. You can't win when your bodies are not aligned. All you can do is lose.

But it wasn't about the Easter clothes. Or the poker. Or the lack of friends and the bad businesses. It was about my baby and eventually learning to be a father.

How to Be a Comedian

"I hope you accidentally drink leukemia at a picnic"

"You have the timing of diarrhea in the 9th inning"

"That's an interesting accent you got there. Are you from stroke-victim?"

The jokes are offensive and depraved. The best comedians are truly twisted humans who have a private truth in the center of their black holes and they have the honesty and skill to share it with us. I can't stop laughing when I read his stuff or see him on TV or in a movie. That's Jim Norton. He's been around the block awhile as a standup comedian but I first saw him (as an adult) on the HBO series "Lucky Louie" (starring my favorite comedian, Louis CK) where he was the disgusting neighbor always popping in and making gross jokes. I couldn't believe it when I saw him. An old man! I watched his HBO special and also his series where he'd bring on other new comedians. I then read his books "Happy Endings" and "I Hate Your Guts".

The first time I heard him do standup-comedy was when we were in 4th grade together. He was the new kid in school. Usually the new kids shut up and kept their head low while the rest of us "veterans" got used to them. Maybe we would be friends with them. Maybe not. I remember very clearly this new kid sitting about two rows from me, his head straight up, and on day one he was non-stop telling jokes and making the class laugh. I couldn't stop laughing. My stomach hurt from laughing so much. I thought I was going to pee in my pants. Mrs. Osborne, the teacher, even said he was a "natural comedian". We all knew even then he was made to be a comedian.

Incidentally, the last and only time I had peed in my pants in school was when I was in first grade. I was trying to hold it in as long as possible. I couldn't figure out how to use the zipper in the urinal like all of the other kids so I would try to wait until I was home. But on this particular day it was too long to wait. "Can I go to the bathroom," I said to the teacher. And I ran out of the classroom straight to the urinal but... "What's wrong," said the kid next to me.

"Too late," I said. And my pants were completely soaked from the urine before I had the chance to figure out the whole zipper/urinal thing. (To this day I've never attempted the urinal again and just use the stall like any normal woman does.) I had to spend the rest of the day in the nurse's office and then my mom picked me up with a new pair of pants. Thank god I'm a grownup now.

I always think I'm funny. When I want to make people laugh with a post, I can. When I want to make people laugh when I do public speaking or I go on TV, I usually can. I always wonder, can I do this straight out – be a comedian? When I was single, right before I met Claudia, I would drink at my favorite restaurant and write down jokes on a pad that I thought I could perform. I'd then call my friend in California who writes sitcom comedy and run the jokes by him to see what he thought was funny. I wanted to be a comedian.

But I can't.

I look back at Jim and the raw talent. Everything he said was funny. He couldn't help himself. 4thgrade was the only time we ever really hung out. He kept trying to tell me "KISS" was the greatest band ever but for me at that time I only listened to Billy Joel, or...Barry Manilow (hey, "Copacabana" could be the best song of all time).

—⚏—

"Two men spit in their hands, help each other out, then laugh about it later. Just to be silly"

"I don't wear rubbers cause you can't catch it twice"

"I am so ugly, if I got a girl pregnant she would throw herself down a flight of stairs"

—⚏—

And yet despite the fact that all of us were constantly laughing whenever he opened his mouth I still read about all the effort, the persistence, the sheer mania, he had to go through in order to rise up in the comedy world. How he studied the greats, emulated them, performed at the crappiest dives, rose up bit by bit despite the hardship. Nothing was easy for him. If he had ever given up, he never would've been the successful comedian we all took for granted he would be. His talent was worth nothing. I was even surprised to read about a suicide attempt when he was 18. I didn't know. I was too busy in my own fantasy world.

—⁓—

"I had AIDS, but I beat it with Advil"

"If I was a girl, I'd have a miscarriage right now"

"Look at that little bloody thump on the floor, that was gonna be something!"

—⁓—

I didn't really know him at all when we were older. I wish I had made more of an effort to make more friends in high school with the people I legitimately liked. But I kept to myself. I played chess. I rode my bicycle in my neighborhood.

I waited for the hell of suburbia to be over, so that real life could begin. The suburban night comes to an end with the locks of the garage doors opening with metallic slowness, the extra-wide roads creeping to life, the pretentious cadillacs moving like reptiles in a fogged line so they can get to the city and begin ordering around the slaves around and climb on their backs to be Vice-Presidents of Something, Inc. They get to work, quickly wash their faces with daylight, their faces becoming pale, pasty, ugly, old, forgotten, in that order, as the humor leaves their bodies with their youth, and only the unlucky ones survive til death with nothing permanent to show for it other than another generation to take their place.

I didn't make too many friends, thinking that one day the exact thing my parents generation worshipped: money, would be mine and I would be finally happy. As a youth I fantasized about the money. And when I had a bit of money, poverty grasped me like a scorned lover and wouldn't let go. I fantasized about the kids that tortured me. They would come to me when we were older, looking for jobs and I would string them along until I finally said "NO!" and they would cry hopelessly. In my head I was as mean and cruel as any kid that tortured me. Now I want my youth back, to reverse those fantasies, to reverse that cruelty, to cure in advance the shame that plagued the next thirty years of my life. To become friends with the people who I had been afraid of.

Maybe Jim tried to kill himself at 18 because he saw the joke before the rest of us did. Jim Norton was funnier by far than all of the kids I grew up with. We were constipated with life and he had crapped it all out. But what made him a comedian was not his enormous talent, or his ability to see through the lies – so easily funnier than the rest of us, but the persistence, mania, tireless study of his peers, and the pursuance of the dream that left the rest of us behind when all we do is weep and sleep.

MOUSE IN THE SALAD

A few months ago I was playing backgammon with Stephen Dubner when we saw something that was so repulsive it almost made me throw up right on the spot. And I thought Dubner was going to pass out because I've seen him do that before in situations that other people might just label "gross" and walk away. Here's the thing about Dubner. He wrote Freakonomics which catapulted him to success. And I think its a great book. I wrote about it on my blog. But here's the reality: I think he's a world-class writer with his other books. "Confessions of a Hero Worshipper" is one of my all-time favorites.

I hope Stephen eventually writes more books like that. I might've even been telling him this (lecturing the best selling writer on writing) while we were eating at Le Pain Quotidien on the upper west side and playing backgammon. He might have even been beating me in that particular moment so the interruption was welcome. Beating me at a game is almost an unforgivable sin but every now and then he gets away with it.

Suddenly, we had to stop the game.

The woman at the table next to us started in with a combination of screaming and crying. It was one of those horrible animal sounds when all the animals around sense something is very very wrong and look over. Here's what was wrong:

There was a dead mouse in her salad.

She moved it from the salad to a bowl. I walked over there and asked her if I could take a picture so she could have it in case she needed it for anything. I was being nice and she thanked me profusely but my real motive is exactly what you are seeing here: I wanted to write about it. I play a humanitarian on TV.

Le Pain Quotidien is a great chain of healthy restaurants. But it's growing fast. When a company grows fast things (mice) literally slip through the cracks. Stephen did a radio show about the situation a few weeks ago. I said on the show: A lot of things have to go wrong in order for that mouse to get there. It's not a simple mistake. A bag of salad had to be left open in a kitchen, unobserved. A mouse had to crawl into it. The salad had to be then shut. The mouse then died. At some point in the future the salad was removed from storage and opened. A hand reached into the bag and didn't watch what it was doing. It pulled out a bunch of lettuce, and one dead mouse, and put it on a woman's plate. All unnoticed.

Things happen from the top down. Its not the waiter's fault. Or the guy in the kitchen's fault. Or the manager's. Somewhere near the top of a fast growing company, an executive can't handle the growth, and doesn't put the structure in place for a mouse to sneak into the salad bag. This happens with every company on the planet. A mouse in the salad means congrats, you are growing. But it also means if you can't handle the growth, you're about to die a horrible death. Trapped without oxygen in a salad bag.

A waiter had to then take the plate, and still not notice the dead mouse that was on it. It was delivered to the woman. The woman began eating the salad. Until she ate enough lettuce to uncover the mouse, or until she stuck her fork in it and picked it up.

Stephen put on his Freakonomics hat. We didn't pay our bill and we packed up our backgammon set and began walking out. "Lets let the manager set the price of the bill for us." At the door, the manager came up to us. Stephen said, "look, we mostly finished our meal but now we don't feel so well, given the mouse thing. What do you suggest we pay for this meal?"

Stephen's theory was that if the manager was good, he would have us pay nothing, even offer us incentives to come back. Stephen's going to write about this when the radio show comes out so I'll let him finish off what the manager said. Apparently, in his article he mentioned that some professor disagreed with his approach.

As we were leaving, the woman who found the mouse in her salad came up to me and said, "Thank you! Thank you so much. You are very kind to help me out here." No problem, I said, I wanted to help. I would hate to find a mouse in my food. I was actually feeling a gag reflex as I was thinking about it. I think I'm feeling that even right now as I write this.

She was still thanking me. "Its very sweet that you would help us. My friend and I eat here regularly. Maybe we will see you when we eat here again next week."

What the...?

Why I Started Stockpickr

I needed some money and all of my current plans were not working out. First off, I was running a hedge fund. But my fund was really a "fund of hedge funds". In other words, I invested in other people's funds.

Which, when you think about, is really a stupid idea. First off, the 12 funds I was invested in were charging me fees and they would "lock up" my money for a year (i.e. I couldn't take the money out for at least one year and even then there were penalties and conditions). Then, I had to turn around and charge fees to my investors and lock them up.

It was really a clusterfuck, pardon my language.

So I tried to sell it. And I had a buyer. A bank. They offered me a nice amount BUT they had one condition: I had to sign a six-year employment agreement. And, if during those six years I ever quit OR if they ever fired me, I had to return all the money and they could still keep the fund. What a bad idea. I was almost crying when I read the agreement because I thought we had a good thing going on. My lawyer even said, "I thought slavery was outlawed".

I did what I always do then. I stopped returning their calls.

They kept calling me every day. Ten times a day, "We can negotiate. Call us back." But sometimes when things are so far apart and someone is clearly trying to pull something over on you then there's no sense in calling them back. They ended up going out of business anyway. Good riddance. I was staying at the Chelsea Hotel the day I got the contract and I remember my business partner, Dan, telling me we can't take this deal. I was still willing to take it. I ended up drinking myself to death in the bar next door, El Quijote. They had to revive me and carry me up to my room at the end of the night. The next day, the bartender, who couldn't even speak English, gave me his uniform he wore the day before. He said, "Here. I owe you." I took it but he couldn't explain why.

But I still needed money. I pitched a major $10 billion hedge fund on an idea I had. Here's the idea: (you can steal it if you want. It's still a good idea): I would take the top 30 best investors: Warren Bufffett, Carl Icahn, etc. and I would buy all of the stocks they own but at discounts to where they bought them. Any big investor has to file every quarter what they own. So I could roughly guess what price they paid. And if Buffett owned Exxon at $100 and it went down to $50 its like Warren Buffett works for me, gave me his full analysis about why Exxon was cheap at a $100 AND I get the 50% discount to what he paid. Thanks Warren! And guess what: I pay Warren nothing for his hard work. BAM!

I would diversify across 30 of the top investors and diversify in every industry and hedge my positions by shorting (betting against) the broader markets. I don't want to get too technical here. But I modeled out the idea and the results were phenomenal. I pitched the $10 billion hedge fund and they loved it. They were willing to start me out with $100 million and build up from there but I had to come in and sit at their office. What??

AND I had to stop all of my writing and all of my other "activities".

I couldn't do it. What if I gave up everything I was doing and then I had a 0% year for some reason. What if, by chance, it was the worst year ever for my system. As risk-taking as I often am, I am very risk-adverse when someone tells me I can only do ONE thing in my life. I didn't want to take the risk of giving up everything AND making no money. At any given time I have to have many things going on. Right now, this second, I am trying about 10 different things. I diversify everything in my life, from thoughts to career changes.

By the way, how do I know this is still a good idea. Because even a year ago I pitched this to a $10 billion+ fund (a different one) and they loved it but I didn't feel like doing it then. Be my guest. Steal it. Make a lot of money. Eat a lot of food. Divorce your wife. Buy a plane. All I ask if you take this idea is that if you ever see me lying in the street with a needle sticking out of my elbow then you give me a twenty dollar bill so I can buy more heroin (not crack. I think heroin makes you happier than crack).

So now I was really desperate for some good ideas. I started unwinding the fund of funds. It was a waste of time. Thank god I started unwinding when I did. Sometimes luck favors the… lucky. I forget the expression. But I'm the luckiest person alive because if I had even waited a few months, and then given the time it takes to unravel one of those things, I would've been stuck in the 2008 mess. Instead, I managed to save all my investors money and avoid the entire crisis.

What to do? I went back to my roots. Creating Internet sites! I could be an entrepreneur again. Whoopee!

I created a site first: keauty.com (the domain long since expired), which was like Facebook but for beauty contest aspirants. I even had a deal with some woman's magazine that I would advertise them if I would become their official online beauty contest. I then added dating site features so people could contact each other. Essentially someone can log in, put up their profile, put down all their interests, and get voted on 0 to 10 about whether they were beautiful or not. And I would give money to the winner each month.

But nobody was signing up. So I tried other ideas. CelebrityKeauty.com. I hired an intern to put up celebrities as if they were beauty contest aspirants. I'd put in their profile, etc. I'd even put in historical figures. It would be fun. The idea is people would check back every day to see who else would be put up. I hired an intern, described what I needed, and just let him go at it. The next morning I woke up to see the first celebrity he put up: Osama Bin Laden. And in the profile he described all the great things Osama Bin Laden had done for his people. I called him up and I tried to be gentle. I didn't want him tracking me down and blowing up my house. I said, "here in America, everybody hates Osama Bin Laden".

He said, "but around the world, many people love him." I said, "but we're in America. You're in America. I'm in America. Let's cater this site to Americans, ok?" But I fired him. The site was no good anyway.

I did lots of contest sites like that. I did one site where people would upload the funniest videos and everyone would vote. I even did SmokeLove.com (see picture above) a dating site for smokers. Then I combined all the sites into one contest site. Then I made it meta: you can make any contest site you wanted. I called it Unlea.sh. I got a media class at Syracuse University to bulk make contest sites. I had about 100 contest sites running. Most beautifulpet. Most delicious recipe. Smartest person, etc. I had two well-known investors who wanted to invest.

But I wasn't feeling the magic. You need magic at some point to know an idea is good. What's magic? It's that feeling you get when everyone is writing you saying, "I can't live without this website." It's that feeling you get when even you think, "I can't live without this website." This service I'm providing is the best service in the world. It's that feeling you get when people are using your site and you love them and they love you. I wanted that feeling. SmokeLove.com wasn't doing it for me.

My business partner said, "well, I guess that was worth a try. Let's cool off now. We've tried ten different ideas and nothing is working." Because we were spending money on every site. It's no good watching your bank account get lower and lower. At a job, you get paid every month or every two weeks. You know what your bank account will be. But our bank accounts were getting lower and remember the first thing I said when I started writing this, "I needed money". My last big deal had been at least two years earlier. And then the IRS paid a visit to my house. They put a sticker on my door. So I needed the money.

For the past 16 years I've only eaten what I've killed. At this point, it's the only thing I know how to do – despite the incredible volatility in that, the fear, the anxiety, the stress – there's also love, and freedom, and happiness.

"One more try," I said. I have this one idea. What if we make a recommendation engine on stocks. It's like what we were pitching that 10 billion dollar fund: lets put up Warren Buffett's portfolio and the portfolios of the top 1000 investors. Then you can put in your portfolio, see who correlates you, and then you get stock picks. So we built that. Then we added more and more things.

We added a feature so that every day, for free, people would see the signals and systems I used to use when I was trading for hedge funds. Then we added forums for community. We added the ability to make blogs about stocks. We added a Q&A system so people could ask each other questions. The one thing we never added was a news feed. How come? Because news, even about stocks, is all lying and bullshit and doesn't belong on any trader's desktop.

In other words, instead of having a $10 billion fund invest with us, we set up all of our strategies for free on a website and added community. And no news. Guess what the headline was a year ago: "Markets worried about Greece!" Guess what the headline is today: "Markets worried about Greece!" The news is BS. They lie to you and manipulate you and, of course, entertain you by tickling your fears.

I didn't want that. Instead I set up my IDEAL investment website. People loved it. I was getting new users every day. I got an email from someone who said, "please block me from your site because I am spending too much time on it." It was the exact website I would use as an investor. And it was profitable from day one (we had advertisers) and I loved almost every moment of it.

And then I sold it.

I don't get attached to anything.

LOTS OF NAKED PEOPLE

Tamara gave me a naked picture of herself. "It's a gift," she said. Our yoga instructor, a pretty blonde girl, was also in the picture. Naked. To be fair they were surrounded by about thirty other naked people. To this day I don't know where to hang it up in my house. Tamara wanted to set me up with the yoga instructor after class. We asked her out to dinner but she said she was busy. "Another time." It was the first yoga class I had ever gone to.

The photograph was taken by my favorite photographer, Spencer Tunick. I wanted to be like Spencer Tunick. Not because he was such a great photographer (although he is). I figured that was a skill that I could learn. But his ability to get thousands of people to take their clothes off for him seemed like a power only a God could give someone. I wanted that power. It was like he could just walk up to someone and say "take your clothes off!" and they would. And he could do that to thousands of people at the same time. He had a pact with Satan. It's hard enough for me to get one girl to take off her clothes.

Tamara and I went to dinner with him. "What's the key to success to being a great artist?" I asked him. And I wasn't pandering. I had done his website a decade earlier when he did a documentary for HBO. I was a huge fan.

"You have to know a lot of people," he said. "And network very well. You have to hustle to get your work shown."

The answer disappointed me then. I thought he was going to tell me something about art. Or photography. Or his mutant powers to control naked women. Like what the keyword was. You say, "Myztplyk and they just take their clothes off". But it was all about who you knew, how you networked with them, and who blessed you from above.

Just like in any other industry.

"You could be the best artist in the world," he said, "but if you don't know anyone then nobody will know you."

A few weeks ago, VC/writer Brad Feld asked on his blog what the best science fiction books of all time were. I noticed many of the answers were books that most of the commenters probably read when they were kids. Books by Robert Heinlein, Isaac Asimov, Roger Zelazny, and Orson Scott Card were the top mentions. Very few mentions of books written since 1990 and only one mention of a book written since 2000. In fact, it was written in the past two years.

Wool.

I happened to meet the author, Hugh Howey, at a dinner Amazon held for self-published authors in Santa Monica the week of the announcement of their latest Kindle release. At the table was a woman who had written and self-published over 100 books. Sitting next to me was Raymond Bean, who had written a bestselling collection of children's books beginning with "Sweet Farts". Hugh was sitting across from me. He was happy.

It was almost as if he couldn't believe his own success.

Just a few months earlier he had worked as a clerk in a bookstore. Now he was being flown all over the place by Amazon. Wool, books 1-5 were all in the top 10 on Amazon's best selling Sci-Fi titles. Since then, #6 and #7 came out. After the trip I read all the Wool books. I also read Hugh's book "The Plagiarist" and "The Hurricane". Ridley Scott has since bought the rights to Wool, the movie, and Random House bought the rights to the hardcover Wool.

The Wool series is the best science fiction I've read. It came out of the self-published world. Just like "50 Shades of Grey" did. I had a chance to meet all of the kindle and createspace people on that trip. They were smart, they were preparing for the future, they were creating the future so authors like Hugh and EL James could start their publishing careers. Nothing like this has happened since the invention of the printing press. That sounds like exaggeration but if you look at the growing numbers of self-published books out there it would astonish you.

"Yeah, but there is still a stigma to being self-published," two people have said to me recently. One was a *NYT* bestselling author. The other was an editor of books published by mainstream editors.

I doubt that Hugh Howey cares about any stigma. I've had 10 books out. 5 by main stream publishers and 5 self-published. Three observations.

A) My bestselling books were my self-published ones.

B) I've made more money on my self-published books. One of my friends who recently self-published told me he's making a living from his one book. He wrote and published his book in the space of two weeks. With a mainstream publisher it will take you two years.

C) The quality (as measured by the reviews on Amazon) is higher on my self-published books.

D) NOBODY has ever asked me, "who is your publisher?" on any of my books. Nobody cares. The only people who care are the ones who benefit from the continuation of an antique industry. It's' like someone from Harvard Law School asking you where you went to law school. It's important to him that he think he's better than you. But it's not important to anyone else.

Louis CK was talking in his latest standup about how "Women get to look elegant in sex" whereas men just climb on top and "ride the dick train". CK is just a non-stop list of truths reeling off for an hour. "When I was 35," he said, "A woman blew me and two years later she hung herself. That's an interesting story." Another line, "Staying married for the sake of the kids is like holding in a giant shit for your entire life."

So he put it all together and instead of waiting for HBO or some other guys in suits to pay him for his Tao-like wisdom, he sold his hour for $5. "Everyone thought people were going to steal," he told Jimmy Fallon, "so I wrote a note and said please don't do that." A day later he had an extra million dollars in his pocket. "I never had a million dollars before."

Louis CK has been in "business" for 25 years. Now he has a million dollars. Or more. Whatever he has. But he got it via self-publishing his work. Nobody in corporate America wanted to give it to him. They wanted him to be their slave. To slowly lose his color over the years until he was a ghost, hanging onto them for scraps of life. But he didn't wait for that. He chose himself.

—⟶⟶—

It's very exciting now. Figure out who you are. Be honest about it. Become effective at communicating whatever your "truth" is.

Then you create, you network, you hustle, you price, you sell, you execute. There is nothing else. Underemployment (where people are either unemployed or hired at jobs they are unhappy with) is over 20% and it's going higher and higher. This is not a fault of the economy. It's because innovations and outsourcing are replacing the entire middle class.

Here's some excuses:

"But I'm not an artist"

"But I'm not an entrepreneur. Not everyone is an entrepreneur".

"It's not all about money, you know."

"I'm too old".

"I'm too young"

"I'm safe in my current job"

"There's a stigma when you leave (mainstream blah blah)."

"Not everyone can do what YOU can do". (I wish someone can tell me what it is I do and how I did it. Because it's taken me 25 years and I'm still trying to figure it out).

"I'm sick."

"I'm sick of you talking about this already."

"I don't have technical skills"

"I tried but I can't do it."

"I need money NOW. I can't put in the work."

"I don't have TIME".

You can hold onto all of those excuses if you want. or pick your favorite and make it your very own. Dress it up for the holidays. Put a little chocolate nose on it. Make the excuse with a smile. I've used most of those excuses also. But all of those excuses can be overcome. Right now you might have the luxury of deciding which excuse you will use. Tomorrow you will have the luxury of using an excuse to explain why the first excuse didn't save you. But pretty soon there will be no excuses.

—⁓—

When I tell the first story to people, the one about the yoga instructor, people ask me, "well, did you ever go out with her?" I have seen her naked after all. And she was pretty. I mean, she was a yoga instructor. So why not? But why does that have to be the first thing people ask? The answer is, no, I did not go out with her. I went out with and married a different yoga instructor instead.

ABOUT THE AUTHOR

James Altucher is a successful entrepreneur, chess master, spiritual teacher, and writer. He has started and run more than 20 companies, some of which failed, several of which he sold for large exits.

But more important, James has been inspiring people through hundreds of events, through his books, and through weekly Q&A Twitter sessions by speaking on topics including stress, fear, anxiety, business, love, money, and relationships.

His writing has appeared in most major national media outlets, including the *Wall Street Journal*, ABC, *The New York Observer*, Positively Positive, Tech Crunch, and Thought Catalog.

His blog, The Altucher Confidential, has attracted more than 15 million readers since its launch in 2010. He is the author of thirteen books; including the national bestseller *Choose Yourself* and *The Power Of No*.

Join him at http://JamesAltucher.com or Twitter @Jaltucher.

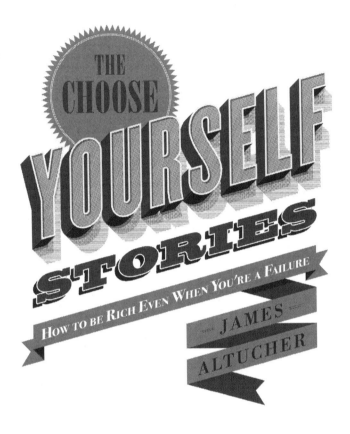

THE CHOOSE YOURSELF STORIES

HOW TO BE RICH EVEN WHEN YOU'RE A FAILURE

— JAMES ALTUCHER —

ISBN-13: 978-1500193416   ISBN-10: 1500193410

Printed in the United States of America
Cover design by: Herb Thornby/Erin Tyler
Interior design by: Erin Tyler

26411828R00162

Made in the USA
San Bernardino, CA
19 February 2019